From Doomed East Prus

From Doomed East Prussia to Tunbridge Wells
A young boy's escape across war-torn Europe

Jane Bakowski

YouCaxton Publications
Oxford & Shrewsbury

ISBN 978-1-913425-16-6
Published by YouCaxton Publications 2020
YCBN: 01

YouCaxton Publications
enquiries@youcaxton.co.uk

This book is dedicated to the memory of
Dieter Teubler's parents,
Erna and Franz.

Contents

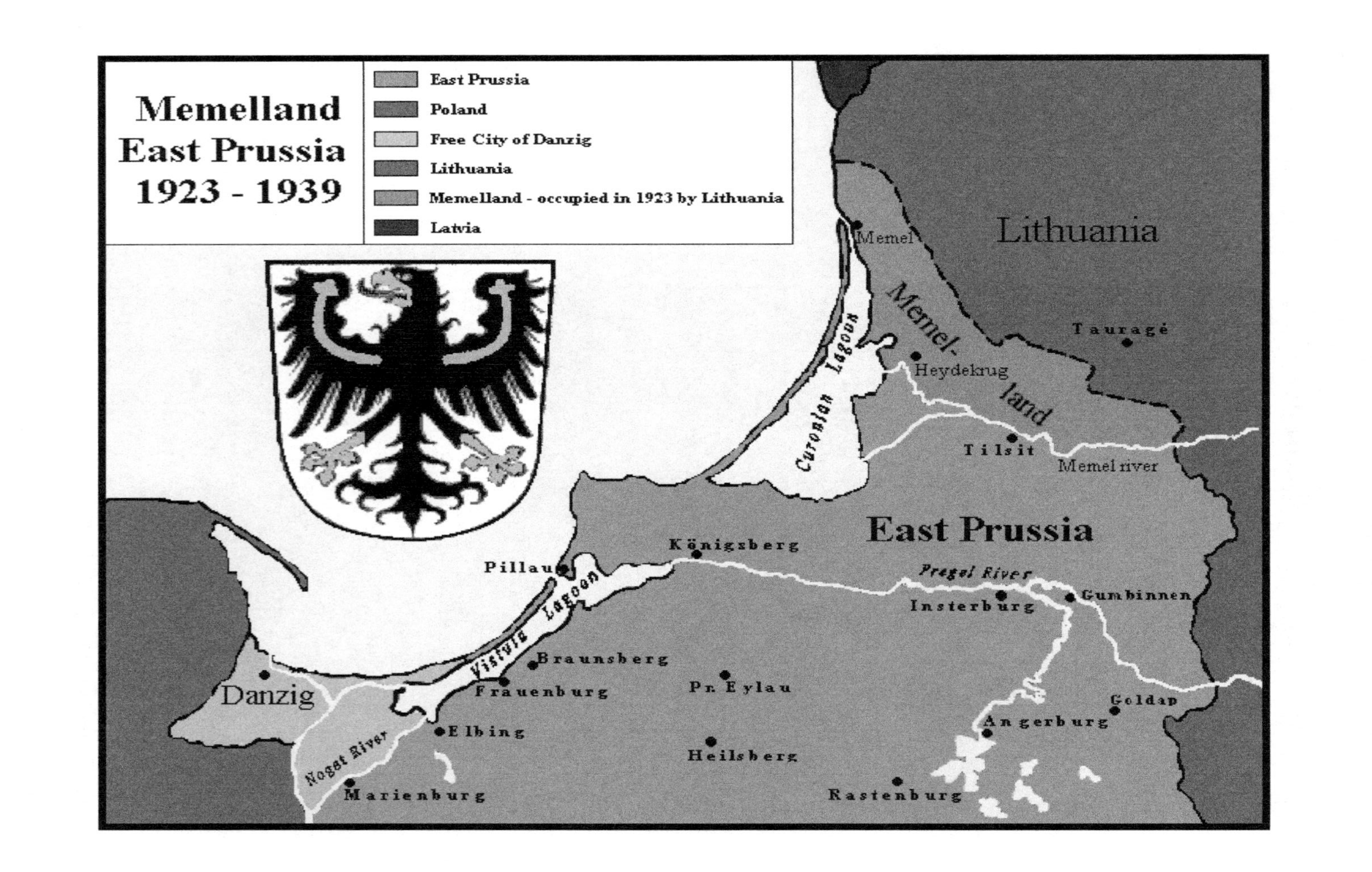
Memelland
East Prussia
1923 - 1939
East Prussia
Poland
Free City of Danzig
Lithuania
Memelland - occupied in 1923 by Lithuania
Latvia
Lithuania
Memel
Memel-
land
Tauragė
Heydekrug
Curonian Lagoon
Tilsit
Memel river
East Prussia
Königsberg
Pillau
Pregel River
Insterburg
Gumbinnen
Vistula Lagoon
Braunsberg
Frauenburg
Pr. Eylau
Danzig
Elbing
Nogat River
Heilsberg
Goldap
Angerburg
Marienburg
Rastenburg

Who in the world has heard of Memelland?

Who can picture the crescent of land, 129 kilometres from top to toe and just thirty-two kilometres wide, which once curved down from the sandy Baltic coast in the north to its southern border nudging the grassy banks of the River Memel? And who knows of the patchwork of farms and forests, neat in the Prussian way, where generations had lived and worked, children following parents following grandparents in traditions stretching back over centuries?

But for Dieter Teubler, the family home on the north-eastern border of this quiet East Prussian backwater was a whole world, a place tethered so strongly to this land that there seemed no reason ever to leave.

Memelland's chief city, the Baltic port of Memel, had been established by the Teutonic Knights back in 1250 and, with its ancient castle, had been part of Prussia for almost seven hundred years, right up to the close of the First World War.

And yet, before his tenth birthday, the young boy would be glancing over his shoulder for one last look at his childhood home as he and his family ran for their lives. For at this late stage of the Second World War, as Hitler's plans for world domination teetered on the edge of ruin, the terrifying cry: "The Russians are coming", was echoing the length and breadth of East Prussia and beyond.

A perceptive and thoughtful boy, Dieter had long sensed his parents' unease as the war drew ever nearer. After all, their farm stood just a kilometre from the border of Lithuania, already under Russian control. As the German/Russian front line shifted back and forth, East Prussia was poised on a knife edge - and everyone knew it.

"We had already packed up our wagon and left once, in the spring of 1944," said Dieter. "But then the Russians retreated and so we returned home. But this time, as I looked back to see my father standing there - he had to stay behind on war duty - I knew I would not see Memelland again for a long time. I was thinking it would be about five years, as a child I just couldn't imagine it being for ever."

For while Dieter would eventually return to visit the site of his old home in the tiny village of Nattkischken, bringing with him his children and grandchildren, by then Memelland itself would be long gone, swallowed up by the re-aligned borders laid down after the war was over.

In the years to come - the ordeal of the long, dangerous trek west in the months following that last glimpse of his home, his family's struggle to build a new life in postwar Germany and his eventual move to England and life as a husband and father - Dieter's natural resilience would be tested time and again. And, as for so many whose lives were turned upsidedown by war, the happy innocence of his early childhood years would remain a golden memory shimmering just beneath the day-to-day reality of his new life.

CHAPTER 1:

CHILDHOOD IN MEMELLAND.

"My father used to carry a revolver with him, just in case. He said: 'We live in border country. When the war is over, we should look for somewhere else'."

Dieter Teubler was born in February 1935 into a world on the brink of catastrophe.

But, dozing in his mother's arms in the family farmhouse in Memelland, the newborn baby could know nothing of the fury about to be unleashed across his homeland. For him, the world of early childhood would stretch only as far as the barn and cowsheds alongside the house, the cornfields beyond the kitchen gardens and the rippling avenue of silver birches heralding the approach to his own village, Nattkischken (now Natkiskiai, in Lithuania).

And even as Adolf Hitler thundered and roared, as munitions factories boomed day and night and Germany's armed forces multiplied, the baby was enjoying his first teetering steps into a quiet, rural world where it seemed little would ever change.

For Nattkischken, on the eastern edge of East Prussia, was as far from Hitler's Berlin, in Germany's western heartland, as from the old Russian city of Leningrad way over to the east, in a region described by one observer as "somewhere on the way to Russia, practically in China".

Celebrated writer Thomas Mann, who built a blue-shuttered summer house in Nidden, midway along the jutting Kurische Nehrung spit, with its pine trees and silvery sand, also stressed his sense of being on the edge. For him, nowhere else in Europe felt so far from Europe as this place where east and west seemed to collide.

But for Dieter, who knew nothing else, his village, with its church, small square and scattering of shops and businesses, was the centre of the universe, a place as familiar to the growing child as his own home, the figures in the landscape almost as familiar as his own family.

"It was the main village in the area, with a church, two general stores, a tailor and a Russian shoemaker with gold teeth. There was also a seamstress who always wanted to be paid in silver coins. She lived with her two sons in a very humble cottage where I sometimes went to play."

Dieter was the first child born to respected local entrepreneur and farmer Franz Teubler and his wife, Erna. Some twenty years younger than her husband, Erna was just nineteen when they married in 1933. The youngest of five children, she was the daughter of well-to-do farmer Otto Bergner and his wife Ella, who lived just a few kilometres away in the small village of Gudden. Her father was also the local Bürgermeister, effectively the mayor, so the wedding between two leading families was a much-anticipated social event. Two dozen landaus processed through the Bergner farm gates that day and, a sign of the families' prosperous connections, no less than six motor cars also drew up outside.

In 1936, less than a year after Dieter's arrival, Erna gave birth to a second son, Peter, followed by two daughters during the war, Doris (1940) and Hanne-Lore (1943).

Alongside the new young family were two other children, Werner and older sister Hildegard - always known as Hilla - from Franz Teubler's first marriage. Their mother, Emma (nee Kenkjleis), had died in December 1929 when the children were aged six and four, and after their father's second marriage they were absorbed into his new family.

"They were slightly distant figures to me as a child because they seemed so much older," said Dieter.

On warm evenings, strolling down through the village, Dieter's father would stop and chat to the village blacksmith, sitting with his family on the cobbled pavement outside their house. A vivid childhood memory would be assisting the blacksmith's daughter, the organist at the village church, when the regular organ pumper was ill.

"I sat out of sight behind the organ, watching carefully as the sensor went down as she played and pumping it up again," said Dieter.

A leading light in Nattkischken was Dieter's uncle, Otto Neumann. Married to his mother's sister, Herta, the quiet, stocky man was destined to play a key role in the family's wartime survival.

"He had come to the village as an apprentice in the shop - he told us he always had to whistle so that the boss knew he wasn't eating sweets - but by now he was a big businessman. He owned a grocery and hardware shop with a pub inside it, sold coal and had a petrol station outside in the square with hand pumps. He had a glazing business, too, as well as running a local bus service."

One of the few people to have a car, a Little Dekaway (later Audi), Otto lived well, regularly entertaining friends and family in his home, separated from the shop by a heavy curtain.

"They had a huge ballroom where we'd sit on the stage with our cousins - Ruth, Horst and Gerda - to watch films, and I remember my aunt sending me to fetch wine for her friends, 'Mosel für die Damen'," said Dieter. "She liked to sit and drink coffee and she wore diamond rings."

With grandparents, aunts and uncles nearby and extended family scattered across the area, the roots of family life in Memelland ran deep.

The Teublers, like thousands of other Protestants, had made the long trek from Austria two centuries earlier to escape persecution. Harassed for generations by Salzburg's Roman Catholic bishops, they had finally been thrown out of their homeland and so, in 1732, the family had set out to make a new life with the generous support of Prussian King Frederick William 1.

Keen to re-populate the wild, swampy area devastated by famine and disease, the king had offered a helping hand to people of all faiths in his bid to make the area prosper. The Teublers were among some twenty thousand Salzburg Protestants who took up his offer, embarking on an exhausting fifteen hundred kilometre trek across the length of Germany. Many would not survive.

Finally arriving in East Prussia, they were confronted by an inhospitable Baltic landscape very different from the shining lakes and high mountain pastures of their homeland. It was a land of freezing winters and short, burning hot summers, a place where bears, wolves and elks roamed a harsh environment seen by Frederick 1's own son, Frederick the Great, as a region unfit for humans.

However the Teublers had always been tied to the land and, freed from years of persecution, they and their fellow settlers quickly set to work to build new lives.

Two centuries later, the formerly wild East Prussia now a byword for neatness, order and efficiency, the family had become respected figures in the local community.

Franz, like his energetic brother-in-law, had established a thriving business, heading the local traders' association as well as running a small farm. But, watching from afar as events in Germany and beyond unfolded, both he and Otto knew all too well just how precarious their situation was.

"A rough track ran from our house to the Lithuanian border, it was very close," recalled Dieter.

"My school was even closer. My father used to carry a revolver with him, just in case. He said: 'We live in border country. When the war is over, we should look for somewhere else'."

For the young boy, Franz Teubler was everything a man should be. Honest and resourceful, he took a leading role in local affairs, was a fair and generous employer and, running his own successful sausage-making business, made sure his growing family was secure and comfortable.

"He was a big personality in a country where people worked hard and drank hard," said Dieter. "Every few weeks he would go off in his horse-drawn cart to buy feed and stock, and each deal would be settled by opening a bottle of vodka or schnapps. By the time he had visited up to ten farms, he would rely on his horse to take him home. I remember our workers would be waiting for him when he got back to lift him out of the cart and carry him inside."

One of the seven children of Hermann and Augusta Teubler, Franz had grown up on a farm about thirty kilometres away in Kullmen Jennen. But, hauling heavy sacks of corn to be ground at the family windmill, watching as a gleaming new railway line was laid across nearby fields, the growing lad had decided early on that he wanted a different life.

"For him, farming was a hobby," said Dieter, whose paternal grandparents died before he was born. "He grew mainly corn, but he was inventive and full of ideas. He had an abattoir and small factory built outside the house for slaughtering pigs and making sausages, and there was a sign outside showing his name and the firm's symbol, a bull's head, which was known by everyone. My mother told me that, at one time, he won a contract to supply the train running from Berlin to Russia with sausages, but that didn't last long because of the war."

As his business grew, Franz Teubler opened three shops, the main branch in Pogegen (now Pagegiai, in Lithuania), the county town, another in Nattkischken and a third in Über Memel, near Tilsit (now Sovetsk, in Lithuania).

"He was always one step ahead," said Dieter. "I remember one very hot summer, the temperatures were in the forties and my father was selling his sausages in the market in Pogegen. There were at least half-a-dozen butchers' stands there, but the only preservative in those days was salt, so they were practically giving their meat away, it was so hot. But my father used to cut ice in the winter and store it in a deep ice house, so that day he had brought big barrels of ice to keep his sausages cool. He was the only one who did that."

Years later, an acquaintance would recall the special taste of Teubler's "hunting sausage", with its haunting tang of garlic.

On another occasion, Dieter and his brother watched in awe as a huge machine rumbled into the farmyard.

"It was making hissing noises and we were quite afraid, we couldn't think what this enormous thing was doing. But it turned out my father had had a pit built in which potatoes were steamed to be kept through the winter. His competitors didn't like it at all! But he liked to experiment and he was a bit of a showman, so that didn't worry him."

However Franz was also a scrupulously fair man and, like the big landowners in grand ancestral homes scattered across the region, he felt a strong moral obligation both to the community and to his own workforce.

"After the harvest, he would let local people go freely into the fields to gather corn heads to make flour or to roast for making coffee," said Dieter.

"A family friend told me later that he often used to take any spare food to the poor families living in very primitive cottages just outside the village."

Keen to make sure his children understood their farming heritage, Franz would demonstrate how, as a boy, he would thresh by hand, holding the corn up high above his head on a windy day to blow out the chaff.

But while Dieter was fascinated by the world around him, watching intently as his parents followed the rhythms and rituals of farm life, he was less keen on being despatched to his mother's parents during the long summer holidays.

"I didn't like it much, there was no-one to play with, and once I was so unhappy that my parents came to collect me."

However Otto and Ella Bergner, presuming, like their son-in-law, that their grandson would continue the family farming tradition, were keen to pass on their knowledge. Sitting around the oil lamp in the evening, Dieter would be given detailed instructions on processing the wool gathered from their small flock of sheep.

"I remember they brought some raw wool in and showed me how to straighten it and take out the dirt before combing it using hundreds of little hooks. After that, granny would spin it. She often sang hymns to herself as she worked, she was very religious."

But although the young boy was always interested in practicalities, he was less impressed by his grandparents' method of fattening up the traditional goose to take centre stage on the Christmas table.

"They opened the barn door and there was this goose sitting in a basket being force-fed. I didn't understand that, I thought it was horrible."

The strange and bloody story of the Bergner pig, slaughtered, in the usual fashion, by being beaten senseless and slit across the throat, also lingered in the sensitive boy's mind.

"I can still hear the sound of the pigs crying when they were slaughtered, I always felt they knew something terrible was going to happen to them," said Dieter. "On that day, they had left a pig for dead, but when they came out it had disappeared. They found it lying under a bush on the other side of the yard, but no-one understood how it had managed to drag itself there."

Frightening stories aside, Dieter, like all the children, revelled in Christmas traditions like the preparation of gingerbread biscuit dough.

"My mother would make it several days before Christmas, then leave it to rest before rolling it out and cutting it into shapes. The biscuits would last all through the season."

However there was one festive tradition which he always dreaded.

"We had to go to the Christmas tree and take a bow, then recite a little poem. I was very nervous that I wouldn't get it right."

As spring buds began to appear through the melting snow, preparations for Easter would begin with the building of nests for the Easter bunny, a task at which young Dieter excelled.

"I was the master builder, using evergreen lined with moss."

At the arrival of Easter, the children would descend on neighbours' houses brandishing silver birch branches and twigs.

Dieter recalled: "We would threaten the ladies by brushing their legs with the twigs and refusing to go away until they had given us 'five eggs, a piece of ham and a slice of cake'."

Home life centred around the kitchen. Small children were bathed in the big wooden tub by the fire, fruit from the garden was made into wine using hefty fermenting jars from the village pharmacy - conveniently near as it was run from a room in the Teublers' own house - and meals were shared around the long wooden table.

"My father grew a lot of cabbages, so every year we made sauerkraut," said Dieter. "That was a great day. The cabbages were shredded in a machine, then dough was smeared around the bottom of a tub to cause fermentation before the cabbage was added in layers with a sprinkling of salt between. A special stamper was used to press it down."

In summer, strawberries and raspberries grown in the family kitchen garden were a special treat and, as the farm's own beehives grew heavy with honey, a farming friend would come to help Franz take off the year's crop and store it in glazed earthenware pots.

Dieter recalled: "We ate very well. We made our own butter, which we liked to spread thickly onto our bread, and every week or so our two maids would make six or eight very big loaves using a large trough. I would watch them in the kitchen pouring warm water into the flour, and when they had finished kneading the dough, they would always save a little bit for the next time."

The loaves were baked in a stone bread oven built into the wall in the laundry room.

"They would carefully weigh the beechwood for the fire - it had to be absolutely correct - then, when the oven was hot, the wood was pulled out, everything carefully swept and the bread put in. It had to be done very quickly to keep the heat in, then the metal door was closed and sealed around the edges with dough."

Describing the children's pleasure in eating the crisp strips of dough peeled away after the bread was cooked, Dieter also recalled with relish the "kukel" - small rolls with a sausage in the middle - sometimes made as a treat for the children.

One of the better-off families in the area, the Teublers employed workers for farm duties and sausage production as well as the two household maids.

Among the regular farm buildings, however, were two metal-lined structures which stood as reminders of the sense of unease which lay beneath everyday life in Memelland.

"They were holding cells," explained Dieter. "Living in the borderland, you never knew when odd people would appear."

For, as events since the end of the First World War had shown, this far outpost of the old German Empire was set amid a viper's nest of conflicting ambitions and old enmities. When Europe was carved up by the Treaty of Versailles in 1919, taking away large chunks of German land, Memelland, with its thriving port on the busy Baltic coast, became an object of desire for both Poland and Lithuania.

In the end, it was decreed that Memel (now Klaipeda, in Lithuania) would become a free international city, overseen by the League of Nations. However a similar arrangement further west in the port of Danzig (now Gdansk, in Poland) created a "corridor" right across Germany, cutting off East Prussia from the rest of the country.

For the German population in Memelland, with Lithuania snapping at its heels and, beyond, the ever-threatening presence of Russia, it gave a further sense of isolation. Just twelve years before Dieter was born, with League of Nations troops distracted elsewhere in Europe, Lithuania had taken the opportunity to move in swiftly to annexe the land it had coveted for so long. Five hundred years of German possession had been wiped out at a stroke and, although Lithuanian sovereignty was to prove short-lived, it was a sign of things to come.

But for Dieter and his brother, their German identity, regardless of outside events, was never in doubt. The ginger biscuits made by their mother each Christmas were German, the solid red brick of the farm buildings was German, and their village and school, apart from the Russian shoemaker, reflected a language and culture which was entirely Prussian.

But, as Franz Teubler so often pointed out to his young son, these were dangerous times, "the silver rattle of fear" voiced by East

Prussian poet Johannes Bobrowski always echoing somewhere in the background.

People discovered wandering in the area were usually held for two or three days in the farm's cells before they were taken away by the authorities but, from time to time, Franz would employ them to help on the farm.

Dieter said: "My mother would give them a hearty breakfast, with plenty of bread and butter, because usually they hadn't had much to eat."

Left in charge of a group chopping wood one day, Dieter's younger brother, Peter, was mortified when one, complaining of a splinter in his eye, disappeared to seek medical help.

"He never came back," recalled Peter.

However one of those taken under Franz's wing was a young Polish man whose role in the family would extend far beyond his farming duties and deep into the war years.

"His name was Stanislaw," said Dieter. "He was only a teenager and my father thought he hadn't done anything bad, so he spoke to the top people and, because of his good name, he was allowed to employ him to work for us."

For the Teubler family, quietly going about their business in their rural backwater, the growing Lithuanian influence in Memelland through the 1930s remained a threat rather than a real influence on day-to-day life. With the prized Baltic port of Memel now in their hands, the priority of Lithuania's leaders was to develop and modernise as swiftly as possible. And although rural Memelland, unlike Memel itself, where Germans accounted for seventy per cent of the population, was predominantly Lithuanian, in far-flung corners like Nattkischken, that meant little.

"For many, the Poles were the people who worked for them, and there was a sense that Lithuanians were a bit strange. I hardly knew any, there were none in our village, but we were brought up not to talk down to them."

However a trip across the border left the boy feeling pity rather than hostility for his neighbours.

"I went with a policeman on his motorbike to help him collect a bicycle from a house just on the other side. That was the first time I had seen anyone with a bed placed on top of the stove to keep warm. He was just an ordinary man. The bike only had one wheel, so the policeman told him he had to fit another, which he did. I felt sad because he lived so backwardly."

Sharing a bedroom, Dieter and his brother slept on high horsehair mattresses under bedding generously stuffed with feathers, a distant memory of warmth and comfort through the long winter months which would haunt him in the harsh winters to come.

"From my window, I could see our neighbour's field. He was a cabinetmaker, and he always had a big window display by his workshop showing kitchen cabinets and furniture as well as oak coffins."

An observant and curious child, the young boy absorbed early on the day-to-day workings of country life.

"I loved it, and I always assumed that I would spend my life on the farm. I think I would have been happy."

However outside events were already propelling him in a very different direction.

All through the 1930s, as Lithuania's determination to force its own language and culture on the region became more aggressive, support for Hitler's Nazi regime, in Memelland and elsewhere, had been growing. At a time when the defeated nation was still struggling from the economic and social effects of the First World War, Hitler's early promises of jobs and good living for everyone seemed to offer a way out. Boys and girls - including Dieter's half-sister, Hilla - clamoured to join the youth movement, with its exciting adventure camps, sport and rousing marching songs, and even many of the better-off saw their Chancellor as a saviour, at least in the early days.

It was hardly surprising, then, that the call for Memelland to be returned to Germany proved so popular. And when Hitler seized control of what he referred to as "the lost province" after issuing an ultimatum to Lithuania in March 1939, soon after Dieter's third birthday, wild scenes of rejoicing greeted the Führer himself when he sailed into Memel on a gunboat the next morning to celebrate his victory. Swastikas hidden away for fear of reprisal were proudly displayed, Nazi flags waved and rousing German marching music echoed across Memel's main square. Lithuania's sixteen-year domination was over, and Dieter and his family found themselves under German rule once again.

Almost nine thousand Lithuanians left when Nazi Germany took over Memelland, adding almost 2,850 square kilometres to Hitler's ever-growing empire, and some thirteen hundred Jews were expelled.

Within weeks, Memel had been turned into a fortified naval base. As later events were to prove, the fate of the population - and of the Teubler family - was thus sealed.

CHAPTER 2:

THE SPREAD OF WAR.

"I heard Uncle Beno say that if the Russians came, he and his wife had agreed that they would kill themselves and their children."

When Hitler invaded Poland on September 1, 1939, taking back the free city of Danzig just as he had seized Memelland, Dieter was four-and-a-half years old and younger brother Peter was three.

Less than a fortnight earlier, Nazi Germany had cleared the way for the invasion by agreeing a non-aggression treaty with Stalin's Soviet Union. By September 3, Britain and France had little choice but to declare war on Germany. The Second World War had begun.

For the two small boys, the news meant little. But as the months passed, life in the quiet, rural backwater began, inevitably, to change.

With eyes and ears always open, young Dieter watched as people came and went, listened to snatches of conversation among the adults and, as ever, observed closely as his father began to make preparations for the hardship he knew would come.

Meanwhile, just after Christmas 1940, the bustling arrival of Aunt Herta signalled preparations for the homecoming of a new baby. Doris was born in Tilsit on December 29 and, watched curiously by her nephew before he was shooed away, Herta prepared a cot for her, slipping in a hot water bottle to stave off the winter cold.

It was the end of a triumphant year for Hitler's armies. After occupying Denmark and Norway they had forged on to take Holland and Belgium before pushing back humiliated Allied forces to the beaches of Dunkirk. They then went on to occupy France in June.

But in Memelland and the rest of East Prussia, daily life was peaceful. The Hitler Youth movement held summer camps and fought mock battles, and at harvest time, prisoners of war, mainly Poles, were brought in to replace the men away fighting.

As the months passed, however, signs of war increased. A year earlier, Stalin had bullied Lithuania and its Baltic neighbours, Latvia and Estonia, into signing an agreement allowing him to set up vital military bases in their countries; within weeks, they had been absorbed into the Soviet Union. For the Teublers, it meant that their most feared enemy was at their door.

But the following summer, the tides of war turned once more.

In June 1941, the self-serving peace pact signed between Hitler and Stalin two years earlier was shattered when Hitler launched a surprise attack on the Soviet Union, declaring: "At this moment, an attack unprecedented in the history of the world in its extent and size has begun."

Having left his Berlin headquarters for a top secret, heavily-reinforced bunker deep in the East Prussian woods, Hitler hunkered down to mastermind Operation Barbarossa. Aiming to extend his empire deep into Russia, the Führer freed his troops of any obligation to observe the rules of international campaign, insisting that "the war against Russia will be such that it cannot be conducted in a chivalrous fashion". He told them: "This struggle is one of ideologies and racial differences and will have to be conducted with unprecedented, unmerciful and unrelenting harshness."

The repercussions of this would be almost unimaginable.

No longer allies, the two nations threw themselves into a bitter war which would leave millions dead and, ultimately, spell the death knell for Hitler's plans. And in Memelland, the war was suddenly much closer to home.

"We looked out of the window one morning to see a slow-moving trail of German tanks and army vehicles going past our house on the main road through the village," said Dieter, recalling the thrilling excitement of that summer day.

"It began at four o'clock in the morning and went on all through the night and the next day. Some of the vehicles had swastikas fixed to the front."

He recalled: "We'd never seen anything like that in Nattkischken. For us children it was quite something to see the cannons and the ammunition, and the army trucks all packed with supplies."

As the convoy rumbled past on its way to Leningrad, while other forces surged across borders to the south to make up a battle front which would slice down through the Soviet Union for almost three thousand kilometres, Dieter and his friends, mimicking the adults around them, saluted and yelled: "Heil Hitler!"

Among the flags displaying Nazi swastikas fluttering all around the village that day was one hoisted on the flagpole outside the Teublers' farm: whatever their personal feelings, failure to do so could have had disastrous consequences.

Excited by the dramatic scene, Dieter sprang eagerly into action when a passing soldier sent him to buy biscuits.

"I ran fast to my Uncle Otto's shop in the village and they filled the bag right up when they heard it was for a soldier, then I ran back and caught up with him - I saw him waving at me from fifty yards down the road."

Also keen to help, Dieter's mother, who was in charge of the local Red Cross group, directed villagers to bring out the fruit juice stored in their cellars to provide drinks for the troops.

"Everyone made their own fruit juice in those days, and it was diluted with water and served from big buckets at the roadside."

Responding to a government order to hand over as much food as possible to support the war effort, Franz Teubler opened up his sausage workshop for the local collection, adding some of his own salamis and butter.

"It was piled from floor to ceiling, and I remember my father was very concerned that the bread would grow mildew if it wasn't collected in time."

Moving steadily east, Nazi forces numbering over three million quickly took over Lithuania, Latvia and Estonia before surging on towards Russia. By Christmas, they had reached the outskirts of Moscow and triumphant Nazi propaganda assured the German public that victory was in sight.

An event which made a lasting impact on Dieter in these unsettled times was the sudden appearance in the village of a young mother, Frau Joswig, and her daughter, Ingeborg. Evacuated from their home in Essen in Germany's industrial heartland on the Ruhr, a target for Allied bombs, their appearance shocked the young boy.

"They looked as if they had just left Belsen, Frau Joswig was like a skeleton," said Dieter.

The unloading of the family's furniture, sent for by the ever-generous Franz Teubler, was equally memorable.

"That was when I saw a washing machine for the first time in my life. It was wooden and worked under water pressure pumped by hand. We had nothing like that. In summer, our white sheets would be washed in a huge tub of water, then laid out on the lawn and left to dry and bleach in the sun."

Along with Ingeborg's ability to walk on her hands, the arrival of her father, a miner, for a weekend stay also left a deep impression on the boy.

"They said he had been a big, strong man before the war, but when the family came to us for a meal, we could see he had been starving. He ate and ate - we stopped counting after he had eaten fourteen slices of bread and sausage."

For Dieter, the Joswigs provided a first, vivid glimpse of a wider, more cosmopolitan world beyond the familiar surroundings of the farm and village.

"They just seemed to appear, it was very refreshing. We could see the huge smoking chimneys twenty kilometres away in Tilsit from the village hilltop, but I had only been away from Nattkischken once, on a two-day trip to Memel, so it gave me a sense of something quite different."

Later that year, as wartime rumours flew, the young boy heard a conversation he would never forget.

"My mother's brother, Uncle Beno, was a farmer. He and his wife, Aunt Ursula, and their two little girls lived in the next village, Kullmen Szaden, and we used to see them at family gatherings."

On that day, the extended family had come together for a christening at an uncle's farm.

"We were all chatting in the sitting room and I remember the priest arriving carrying a big cross," said Dieter. "That was when I heard Uncle Beno say that if the Russians came, he and his wife had agreed that they would kill themselves and their children. There was always the feeling that the Russians were at the gate."

He added: "My father had served in the trenches in the First World War; in the final stages of the second, although he would be fifty in 1943, he eventually joined the army again because he knew that if he served in the Home Army, the Russians would cut them to pieces."

As stories began to emerge in the months following the end of the war in 1945, Dieter and his family would be deeply shocked to learn that his uncle had, as he promised, killed himself and his family somewhere in Pomerania.

"When we left on the long trek, they were probably a few days behind us. I presume he must have shot his wife first, then the children, before killing himself."

By Christmas 1941, an early and even harsher Russian winter than usual had taken its toll on German troops meeting far more resistance than had been predicted by their leaders. Assured that the Soviet invasion would be accomplished in two or three months, they found themselves poorly-clad and with supplies running low. Things were not going as planned, although Nazi propaganda back home still assured the civilian population that victory was just around the corner.

For the Teubler family, the usual gathering around the Christmas table that year was given extra significance by the presence of Werner. The teenager had left his job as a trainee at a department store in Tilsit two years earlier at the beginning of the war to join the navy, so his return must have been cause for an added sense of celebration.

A photograph taken by Erna shows the family seated around the Christmas table in their comfortable dining room, the grandfather clock in the corner alongside a festive tree decorated with stars and baubles.

Werner, a little self-conscious in his smart uniform, sits between his father and his sister, Hilla, cradling baby Doris on her lap. The boys face each other across the table, Dieter alongside his father and young Peter with his mother. It could be any family, anywhere, gathered together to celebrate Christmas, but at this time, with the future unknown, their happiness at being together must have been tinged with apprehension. And as future events would prove, their fear was well-founded.

Watched attentively by six-year-old Dieter, his mother, a keen photographer, had hung a broom across the door that day to hold her camera, then darkened the room, lit a fuse connected to the camera and rushed back to her seat.

"There was an explosion and the room lit up," recalled Dieter who, over half-a-century later, would have the pleasure of seeing this much-treasured family picture on the cover of Memeler Dampfboot - Memeler Steamboat - the popular magazine focussing on memories of his lost homeland.

As spring 1942 turned into summer, the Teublers, like everyone else, had to rely mainly on rumour to try and work out what was really going on. However a conversation which took place in their garden that summer would remain with Dieter for the rest of his life.

He recalled: "My parents were very sociable, they liked entertaining, and on that day they were sitting outside chatting to two German officers. My mother told me later that one took my father aside and said: 'You'd better leave – get out of here.' He was almost warning us, in 1942, that the war was already over and, mentally, I do feel that that was when the war was lost."

On another occasion never to be forgotten, a tall, thin man came to the house asking to speak to Dieter's father.

"He was a baker, he was carrying a lot of bagels and I was pleased because he gave me some," said Dieter. "It wasn't until many years later that I realised he must have been Jewish. I knew there were Jewish people in big towns like Memel, but I had never met any where we lived."

As the two men fell into deep conversation, the boy watched and wondered. A week later, he found the answer.

"Investigating, as boys do, I went into the garage and there was a beautiful car. It was a Wanderer and it looked brand new, with that lovely new car smell."

He recalled: "It belonged to the baker. He had been negotiating with my father to take it, presumably to hide it away, but father told him that was impossible. No-one was allowed to have a car in the war, they had to be given to the Government, so the baker dismantled the engine and took the tyres off to immobilise it."

The Teublers had never had a car, just a transport wagon, and even that had to be sold as the family business declined during the war and the shops in Pogegen and Über Memel closed.

However they did have a landau for visiting friends and family and, most exciting for the children, a troika sledge pulled by two horses, a glorious sight as it whisked through the snowy landscape, bells on the horses' collars jingling.

"It was very smart, it had two rows of seats covered in velvety blue material, with dangling cords, and our uniformed driver would sit up at the front," said Dieter, recalling a magical homecoming through the silent forest from a family christening.

"It was wonderful. I can still hear the bells echoing through the night."

At the age of six, Dieter started at the village school, a purpose-built red brick building close to the Lithuanian border. It was an unhappy experience, made worse by his dyslexia, not a widely-recognised problem at the time.

"It was wartime and the staff were not really qualified teachers. We wrote on slates and we were taught old German script at first. It was quite difficult, the letters were different, and then after a couple of years it was changed to modern script. I still remember how confused I was, and how I would panic when the teacher asked me something."

The sense of confusion - he also struggled with maths - would last throughout Dieter's school life. Despite his struggles, however, he retained a strong conviction that he would succeed in life.

"The Teublers had been thrown out of Austria two hundred years earlier and were among thousands of Protestants who made their way to East Prussia. It was a long hard journey, but they always had self-belief and they could turn their hands to anything. Memellanders were very versatile, extremely capable. I was ambitious, and I never doubted that I would make something of my life."

Never a very robust child - he was much smaller than his younger brother - Dieter's coughing fits worried his mother so much that, concerned that he may have whooping cough, she arranged for him to have an X-ray in Tilsit.

"It was probably the only X-ray machine for miles around and this was wartime, so I think she probably only managed it by putting a piece of smoked salami on the counter - that went a long way in the war! I had to sit up on the huge machine after drinking a pink solution. The doctor said there was a slight shadow on my lung but reassured my mother that it wasn't serious."

As farmers, the Teublers had access to better food supplies than many others. However Franz, ever conscious of the need to set an example, insisted that his family must not be greedy in these hard times. Which is why, waking on the morning of his seventh birthday, in February 1942, Dieter was astonished to see the little round table next to his bed stacked with gifts.

"I couldn't believe it. There were so many that the maid decided to pick up the whole table and carry it downstairs."

However she went down through the house and out through the shop and, as it was a Saturday, had to push through lines of waiting customers.

"My father was serving, and I could feel that he didn't like at all - it was wartime and he thought it wasn't right to display this show of presents."

However there was the odd occasion when Franz allowed his children a small treat, all the more precious for its rarity.

"He took us to the dairy in the next village. His friend was in charge, and he led us down to see where the cheeses were stored and gave us a slice of cheese each with a slab of butter. It was heaven to eat, we loved it."

The golden memory of that rich, creamy Tilsiter cheese, originally created by Swiss settlers in Tilsit more than a century earlier, with its characteristic yellow rind, its cracks and holes, would remain with him.

As 1942 drew to a close, an event long-dreaded by his family became reality when Werner was killed in a freak accident. Serving on the oil tanker and supply ship the Uckermark, previously the well known Altmark, when it docked in Yokohama, Japan, that November, he was helping to clean and repair the ship's tanks when he was caught in a chemical blast. The ship was ripped apart, and Werner died alongside fifty-two shipmates, aged just nineteen.

"That was the first sadness in my life," recalled Dieter, by this time almost eight years old. "The postman came carrying a big brown envelope and my father was taken into a room and given the news that Werner had been killed. He gathered the family together to tell us. We cried all day."

The following summer, quite unexpectedly, they would hear the full story.

Dieter recalled: "My father and I were heading home in our horse and cart one day when we saw a sailor in uniform carrying a big pack. My father stopped and offered him a lift, and he said he was going to Nattkischken to look for the Teubler family."

The young sailor turned out to be a close friend of Werner's. They had agreed that, if anything happened to one of them, the other would do his best to go and see his family. On the day of the explosion, Werner's friend had gone ashore so had avoided the blast which ended his friend's life.

Dieter recalled: "He and my father talked for hours that day."

He added: "I remember Werner had his own pigeon loft in the roof at the farm. After he died, it just went."

As was customary in Nattkischken and elsewhere, bells in the church were rung to mark the death of a local inhabitant. On the Teubler farm, however, the howls of their St Bernard dog chained in the yard drowned out the sound. Concerned that his son's death had been overlooked, Franz Teubler hurried to the church to complain and, a mark of the respect in which he was held, the bells were pealed again for his own ears.

"It was strange, it was as though the dog knew something had happened," said Dieter.

With fathers and sons, cousins and schoolfriends away fighting, notification of local men killed, injured or missing had become a regular part of day-to-day life. In this atmosphere of heightened emotion, the arrival of a young man on horseback to ask for their daughter's hand in marriage must have evoked mixed feelings in Franz and Erna Teubler.

"Walter Allisat came from a farming family. I was impressed because his horse seemed huge, it was dark and gleaming," said Dieter. "My father agreed, but after he joined the army we didn't see Walter for at least two years."

1943 - the year which would bring the threat of Soviet invasion ever closer as the eastern campaign dragged on - began with the arrival of a second baby girl. Hanne-Lore was born on January 22 in Tilsit and, recalled Dieter, her birth, like that of her sister, Doris, triggered a flurry of preparation by his Aunt Herta.

A few weeks later, there was a special celebration when Franz Teubler himself took a few precious hours away from the harshness of everyday life to mark his fiftieth birthday in traditional style.

At six o'clock on the morning of March 24, the great and the good of the village - the Bürgermeister, the bank manager, the miller and a handful of other local men - gathered at the farm and climbed the stairs to stand outside Franz and Erna's bedroom to sing their greetings.

"They sang songs like 'Alle Tage ist kein Sonntag' - Every Day is not a Sunday - for about twenty minutes," recalled Dieter. "Then they all went into the big room downstairs for breakfast and schnapps before going off to work. I remember my grandmother had come over to help get all the food ready."

By the time Franz's next birthday came around, any doubt that the family would have to leave their home to escape the Russian onslaught would have dissolved.

With so many staff and workers away fighting, Dieter's mother set out for Tilsit one day to recruit a maid to help with the house and children.

"She picked Bronislawa Deptula from a group of Polish girls. She was about seventeen, and she and our other maid lived up in the attic. Broni made a great impression on me. She was like a friend, she played games with us and shared food parcels from her parents in Poland."

However a trip home to see her family brought a sudden end to Broni's life with the Teublers. She failed to return and, hearing nothing from her, they feared the worst, leaving Dieter very sad.

"She never came back and I always wondered what had happened to her."

It would be many years before he learned the fate of his old friend.

By autumn 1943, rumours of a Russian invasion were growing stronger by the day. Reports that Stalin's armies were advancing towards the border filled the local population with terror, and many wanted to leave.

However it was not until the following spring, as the German army's final inglorious retreat from the Soviet Union began, that the Teubler family decided the time had come to move.

However the decision was fraught with danger for, although the German authorities had already drawn up detailed evacuation plans for parts of East Prussia, leaving without permission, or even making preparations to flee, had been strictly forbidden. Anyone caught doing so was seen as defeatist and could be instantly shot, a policy enforced by the Nazi local governor, Erich Koch.

A key figure in life in Memelland and far beyond throughout the war, Koch was one of forty-four Gauleiters, or regional Nazi party leaders, appointed by Hitler himself. With little interference from above, their responsibilities were wide-ranging and their powers seemingly almost unlimited.

Writing in "Flight Across the Ice: The Escape of East Prussian Horses", Patricia Clough describes Koch as "a short, stocky railway clerk...with no professional qualifications but immense cunning, criminal energy and an insatiable thirst for power and possessions".

Quickly dubbed "King Erich", Koch lived lavishly and, replacing East Prussian politicians and functionaries with his own henchmen, enjoyed total power across East Prussia, reputedly so shocking even leading Nazis with his cruelty and oppression that some protested to Hitler himself. However Koch's power only increased when he was made Governor of Ukraine and neighbouring Polish districts, extending his empire from the Baltic to the Black Sea. He was destined eventually to die in a Polish prison, but during the war years his power seemed invincible.

But for the Teublers and many other families, the imminent threat of Russian invasion left no choice but to plan their escape: the alternative was unthinkable.

Always planning ahead, Dieter's father had already overseen the transformation of a hay wagon into a sturdy transport vehicle with a wooden roof and sides, over-hung at the front to keep passengers dry and with a small window at the back.

And so, as the long Memelland winter gave way to spring, the family set out with heavy hearts, praying for a swift return.

"We loaded up the wagons to the top with clothing, goods and corn for the two horses and then my mother and us five children headed for the River Memel," said Dieter.

"Before we left, my father had taken away all the animals and let them loose - cows, pigs, ducks and chickens - so that the Russians wouldn't get them."

Before leaving, Erna had also hidden away carefully-wrapped crystal glasses and other valuables, many of them wedding gifts.

Looking back to that momentous spring day, Dieter recalled: "I wasn't frightened because we still believed we were winning the war, so we would be able to return home in a few weeks."

For the first two or three nights, the family camped out in a cow barn some twelve kilometres from Tilsit, but then their father, outraged at his family's uncomfortable conditions, persuaded the manager at Gut Schopenau, a large farming estate nearby, to provide them with a room.

"After that we went to stay with a relative from the Bergner family, my great-aunt, who had a farm in the area."

For Dieter, it was an entry into a very different world.

"I remember my father arranged it by phone, they were very advanced there. That was where I saw my first central heating system - our house was heated by wood and coal briquettes, so this seemed very sophisticated."

He added: "I clearly remember one lovely evening. For some reason, we were not allowed in the garden, but I found out that my aunt was having a bath behind the lilac trees. My uncle was filling it using hot water from the boiler in the kitchen."

After a few weeks of uncertainty and rumour, the desperately-hoped-for news of a Russian retreat finally came through. Deeply relieved, the family decided to return home.

"The house was more or less as it had been," said Dieter. "But father was amazed when one of our cows returned - he had cut a 'T' into her neck, so he knew she was ours. He couldn't quite believe it."

The months that followed offered a brief respite from the fear of invasion as day-to-day life resumed and the sociable Teublers entertained soldiers and friends. However it was not to last. By autumn, they were on the move again.

In early October, as the Russians advanced once more, the order to pack up and leave finally came. And this time it would be for good.

Chapter 3.

THE TREK.

"I knew there was no way out of East Prussia except over the ice."

On the golden autumn day which would signal the end of his old life, Dieter was playing with his friend Hans, the village seamstress's son, in their cramped cottage just up the hill from his family's farm.

He recalled: "I happened to glance out of the window, and I could see a lot of movement outside our house. My mother was rushing here, there and everywhere."

Realising a fresh drama was unfolding, he ran home to the news that the family was on the move again. The date was October 7, 1944. The Russians were swarming towards the East Prussian border in huge numbers and, as the clocks struck noon, the order had gone out to leave Memelland immediately. They were fortunate: as Hitler's refusal to admit defeat hardened, it would be many weeks before Gauleiter Koch bowed to the inevitable and extended the evacuation order to the rest of East Prussia.

"My mother was sweating as she loaded up the wagon, she was in such a tizz," said Dieter.

"I could hear bombardment going on about 130 kilometres away, and if you put your ear to the ground you could detect rumbling. I wasn't frightened, it was something new. One didn't realise terrible things could happen, I couldn't visualise it."

At the end of that long afternoon, Erna left the farm for the last time with her children, nine-year-old Dieter, Peter, aged eight, Doris, three, and baby Hanne-Lore, not yet two. Dieter would never see his boyhood friend again.

"It was about five o'clock. Before father saw us off down the hill from Nattkischken, he had given us a pole to stop the two horses and the wagon colliding, as we didn't have brakes. I watched him as I sat on the wagon, I liked the technicality of it. He stayed behind with some other people to look after things, and to stop pilfering by refugees moving through."

Driving the wagon was the faithful Stanislaw, a familiar figure through much of Dieter's childhood. Along with food for the family and their horses, plus a cow and a clutch of chickens, Erna had packed what clothes and possessions she could, with blankets and fur rugs to stave off the increasing cold. Also tucked in, alongside fine wine and brandy brought home for his family by Werner, were smoked hams and chunks of the celebrated Tilsit cheese.

"My brother and I were wearing our best clothes, the sailor suits we wore to school," said Dieter.

Looking over his shoulder as his home faded from view, he told himself, "we won't be coming back for a long time".

Over seventy years later, he said: "At that age, I thought it would be at least five years, but it turned out to be more than fifty."

Some 500,000 people left East Prussia that autumn. By late January, the number would have swelled to two million.

Dieter learned later that his father, returning to the farmhouse, found a German soldier playing Beethoven on the family's much-prized grand piano, a Blüthner which had been a wedding present from Erna's parents.

"He said to my father: 'You're not going to leave this piano here, are you?'. But my father pointed out: 'I can't take it on my back'."

After sitting for a moment to listen to the comforting sound, Franz Teubler quietly got up and left.

The family joined a seemingly endless stream of wagons and army vehicles moving through the familiar fields and farmhouses towards the distant chimneys of Tilsit, just across the River Memel.

"Everyone was heading in the same direction, all westwards, with more joining from side roads all along the way. People looked thoughtful, rather stunned."

The first stage of the journey was uneventful, but painfully slow as military vehicles took priority over the civilians desperately seeking safety. Stray cattle added to the confusion.

Leaving Memelland for the last time across the famous Königin Luise Brücke (Queen Louise Bridge) spanning the River Memel into Tilsit - the vantage point from which Adolf Hitler had gazed triumphantly at his latest conquest just weeks before the outbreak of war - Erna and her children left behind all that was familiar, trusting to chance to find a safe place to stay as darkness quickly descended.

"We came to a farm and they allowed us to stay for the night," said Dieter, recalling how, in the wide world beyond the River Memel, he soon began to discover wonders he had never experienced.

Clambering down from the wagon, the boy, curious as ever, took the opportunity to explore this new place. And in one of the farm buildings, he soon found something beyond his experience.

"There was a little box in the wall with wires leading from it. When I asked the farmer what it was, he explained that it was an electrical socket. We had electric lights at home, but everything else was mechanical. My father used diesel to power the sausage machines, but here they were so advanced, they could use electricity to drive their equipment. I said to myself how backward things had been at home."

Passing on through the small, historic town of Friedland (now Pravdinsk, in Kaliningrad) on the banks of the River Lava, Dieter was in for another shock.

"It was a lovely town, with a special little train that looked like a bus but ran on rails, but what really impressed me was the hydro-electric power system and the reservoir, I'd never seen anything like that before."

On October 16, just nine days after the family's flight from Nattkischken, long-held fears of a Russian invasion finally came true. It proved short-lived, but widely disseminated stories of Russian brutality in the East Prussian villages as the Red Army surged over the border sent waves of terror across the region. In what would later become known as the Nemmersdorf (now Mayakovskoye, in Kaliningrad) Massacre, reports of the torture, rape and brutal murder of civilians in the small village struck a note of almost unimaginable horror, and convinced most inhabitants that there was no time to lose in getting away.

However Hitler and his war leaders thought differently. For them, any notion of running away was unacceptable, and those who disobeyed faced harsh punishment, even death. Within two weeks, the Russians had been forced to retreat and, determined to bolster resistance, the Nazis sent in film crews to document the atrocities, inviting foreign observers as further witnesses.

Shown in cinemas across the country, shocking scenes in the resulting documentary were designed to harden public and military resistance to the Russian threat. And while accounts of crucifixions on barn doors, beheadings and the brutal murder of babies were later questioned, there was no doubt that the Russians, with the strong encouragement of their leaders, were pumped up and out for revenge for their own suffering at the hands of Hitler's armies. Preparing his troops for the invasion, one army officer, following orders from Stalin himself, had told them: "The time has come to settle accounts with the German fascist scoundrels…we will take revenge for everything."

Meanwhile, the Teublers, like so many others, just kept going. Often bumping into friends and acquaintances heading in the same direction, the family heard that their grandparents, with Aunt Herta and cousins Ruth and Horst, were heading for the small village of Schwönau, beyond the bustling old garrison town of Bartenstein (now Bartoszyce, in Poland).

Moving slowly west towards them, their cow still plodding steadily behind the wagon, Erna and her children rested for a few days at a school. For Dieter, it provided yet another eye-opening experience.

Impressed by the school's vast entrance hall and jumping gleefully down the flight of steps outside with his brother, he thought back wonderingly to his own small village school in Nattkischken.

"You couldn't compare it."

One day, the family was happily surprised by the unexpected arrival of Franz. He had picked up news of their whereabouts, and brought with him a cooked goose, a rare treat. The reunion, however, was all too brief.

"My father had made up his mind to join the army," said Dieter. "My mother couldn't understand why he had done that - he was over fifty so he hadn't yet been called up."

However Franz's decision was triggered by Hitler's raising of a people's militia, the Volkssturm, that autumn forcing all able-boded men between the ages of sixteen and sixty to join in the desperate final struggle. Knowing that the Red Army was likely to be surging through Nattkischken before long, presumably bent on revenge, Franz had decided the lesser of two evils would be to enlist in the regular army.

For Erna and her children, however, the only choice was to keep heading west.

The Christmas season brought a sense of relief and respite as the family was reunited with Erna's parents in Schwönau. Otto and Ella Bergner had managed to find a room in a nearby farmhouse, and Dieter's Aunt Herta and her children were staying in a former guesthouse in the village. His step-sister, Hilla, also joined them there. Working in Tilsit as a butcher's assistant, she had opted to leave Memelland with her employer, so her appearance was a welcome relief.

"It felt quite far away from where things were happening," said Dieter. "We were living in a farm worker's apartment with two bedrooms and it was very comfortable. The windows had wooden shutters, something quite new to me, and it made it much warmer. We even had a Christmas tree, and my mother and sister made wine in a big red enamel milk churn. They felt secure."

Meanwhile, his Aunt Herta, whose older daughter, Gerda, was in the army, was continuing to enjoy small luxuries from her old, comfortable life in Memelland.

"They always had good coffee, even in Schwönau," said Dieter, who later learned that his aunt had had the family's gold watches sewn into corsets to try and keep them safe - unsuccessfully as it turned out.

But while a return to a more normal routine was welcome, Dieter and his brother were less impressed by their enrolment in the village school, where a very elderly teacher had been brought in to replace younger staff away fighting.

"The only thing I can remember is that he taught us how to cut a toenail - he said you must always cut it straight across to avoid in-growing toenails. I've remembered that all my life, but that is all, because I was always more interested in going outdoors to play in the frozen stream."

By January 1945, the family had been in the village for some two months. The year had begun with a New Year's Day radio address, apparently by Adolf Hitler himself, which, although it gave no details on the progress of the war itself, included a ringing declaration that the battle would continue until it was won.

But even as his mother and grandparents continued to hope that the Russians would be pushed back yet again and they would be able to return home, Dieter himself was haunted by the growing belief that this would never happen. Memel itself, for so long Memelland's busiest city, had been under siege by Red Army troops for weeks; by the new year, all resistance would have been crushed and the once bustling streets would be practically deserted.

Always aware of the weight of responsibility resting on the shoulders of his young mother, Dieter was clear that "without my father, I was the man, and I was very anxious. Walking over the fields, we could see people fleeing, the line of horses and wagons seemed never-ending".

Watching the disordered stream of humanity passing by, listening to the constant sound of guns and rockets, the boy soon came to recognise the distinctive roar of Russian bombers flying overhead, "quite different from our planes".

But although the inevitability of invasion was clear to him, he was shocked to realise that not everyone had his foresight.

"I ran to my grandfather every day and said: 'We must leave!', but nobody wanted to go, I couldn't shift either my grandparents or my mother. And when we did, it was almost too late."

Gauleiter Eric Koch - who had already planned his own escape - would finally give the long-awaited order for the whole of East Prussia to evacuate on January 20, 1945. However it came far too late for the planned orderly evacuation for, despite Koch's threats of severe punishment, by then many were already on the road. In the bitter cold of the Prussian winter, thousands of fleeing civilians - mainly women and children, along with elderly men - mingled with retreating soldiers and army vehicles in scenes of desperate chaos.

Eventually, as the front moved back and forth, Erna agreed with her son that it was time to go. By now it was mid-January and, despite the news blackout, persistent rumours that the Russians were closing in were spreading.

However the family had lost their early advantage by lingering so long. Hoping to escape by train to Königsberg (now the city of Kaliningrad, in Russia), with its rail and shipping routes to the west - little knowing that the Red Army was just days away from the city - the family said their goodbyes, grabbed what bags they could and headed through the forest by horse and carriage to the nearest station.

"It took about forty-five minutes, but when we got there the train was absolutely packed with people, we just couldn't get on," said Dieter. "The situation seemed hopeless."

Taking pity on the young family, the station mistress invited them into her house and fed them bacon and eggs before seeing them off on the return journey to Schwönau.

"My grandparents were surprised to see us, but as soon as the front moved back, we left again."

This time, realising travel by train was almost impossible, they set out overland.

"We went with Aunt Herta and our cousins, Ruth and Horst, in their wagon because it was fully enclosed and much warmer."

Big and solid, with rubber tyres, Otto Neumann's old delivery wagon had been a familiar sight back home in Nattkischken.

"My grandparents weren't ready to leave yet, they followed a day or two later with their son Erich's wife, my Aunt Lischen," said Dieter. "We discovered later they travelled a long way by wagon, so their progress was much slower."

He recalled: "It was such a cold night when we left. We were all sitting on boxes in the wagon, and Stanislaw was riding alongside us in our own wagon, carrying our possessions."

The cow, which had provided the family with much-needed supplies of milk during their journey as well as a reassuring link with their old, comfortable life had, reluctantly, to be left behind.

"One night we stayed in a cow barn. My mother was very practical and luckily she was a farmer's daughter, so she was always looking for this kind of place. It meant we would be warm and, by getting up quietly at four o'clock in the morning, she could milk the cows before the maids came down so that we children had milk to drink."

The maids, usually Polish women sent to work on German farms, were often the only people left on these farms after the owners had fled.

But as they moved slowly westwards through the shortening winter days, snow-covered fields glowing silvery-white on moonlit nights, the family huddled together in the wagon were startled one afternoon by a loud crash.

"A German tank had hit us and pushed us into a ditch. Everyone slid down to the floor and Hilla, who had been holding Doris on her lap, lost a front tooth," said Dieter. "Apart from that no-one was hurt, although I'm sure my mother panicked. She had been wearing her favourite heavy amber necklace, but it shattered in the crash and there was no time to gather it up."

Fortunately the solidly-built wagon had suffered little damage but Erna, furious at the danger posed to her family by their own army, immediately confronted their commander.

"She told him we didn't know how long it would take to repair the wagon, and that she and her children needed a lift. He said he could only take us as far as Mehlsack (now Pieniezno, in Poland), about fifteen miles away, but our aim was simply to head west so we accepted."

Before they left, Dieter's mother took what they could carry from their own wagon, then instructed Stanislaw to drive on, hoping to meet up with him later.

"We never saw him again," said Dieter. "He was a good chap. I remember my father presented him with a watch to thank him for his services, something quite unknown at the time, but he liked to treat everyone the same."

In an attempt to help the young Pole survive the war, Franz Teubler had also given him a signed and stamped reference, explaining who he was and where he came from.

Leaving her sister and her children behind to wait for their wagon to be made roadworthy again, Erna shepherded her family onto the army vehicle and set off.

They arrived in the old Prussian town of Mehlsack, with its cathedral and wide streets, to find most of its inhabitants hurriedly packing up to leave.

"We were always on the look-out for somewhere to stay," said Dieter. "I remember one night we stopped at a gasworks alongside huge gas cylinders. I was afraid that if they were hit by a bomb we would all be blown up as well."

In Mehlsack, however, they were lucky to come across a family busily loading up their wagon.

"They were leaving their flat and they told us we could move in when they'd gone. That's how desperate things were, people didn't mind someone else taking possession."

But staying put was never an option. With Allied bombs raining down on the area, the danger was clear. But where to go? Königsberg was no longer possible - it had been surrounded by Russian forces on January 24. However the overland route to the ports of Danzig and neighbouring Gdingen (now Gdynia, in Poland), where refugee ships taking part in Germany's Operation Hannibal evacuation programme were waiting, was also blocked, for the Red Army had completed its encirclement of the area by reaching Elbing (now Elblag, in Poland) on the southern shore of Frische Haff, one of two long Vistula lagoons running alongside the Baltic.

With both escape routes cut off, there was only one last desperate chance of reaching the west - by crossing the frozen waters of Frische Haff. Separated from the sea by Frische Nehrung, the long, narrow strip of land long used by fishermen and holidaymakers, it had been a useful shortcut for generations of local people during the winter months.

"The Red Cross were helping people to get there," said Dieter. "They gave us a sledge and we set off, but it was bitterly cold, it was unbelievable, we couldn't stop our teeth chattering."

In the end, realising that her children were unlikely to survive in such conditions, Dieter's mother told the driver to take the next turn-off and head for some lights she could see across the fields.

"After about half-a-kilometre, we came across a farmhouse," recalled Dieter. "It was quite extraordinary, it was full of people like us, looking for shelter, but my mother told the owner we would all die if we stayed outside any longer, and somehow she managed to find a little room and food for us."

Even more extraordinary was the discovery of a distant relation and her two daughters in the house.

"My mother told the farmer's wife our story and she pointed out the family, who came from the same area as us. We were so surprised."

After a few day's respite, however, it was time to move on, for danger was all around.

"We could see the main road in the distance, and one day Hilla, Peter and I decided to go up and have a look," said Dieter. "But we never got there because two Russian planes came over. It was quite dramatic, they suddenly appeared and we threw ourselves into the snow. They were shooting at us, we found the shells, but they were far too high up to hit us and they never came back."

Erna had arranged for her family to travel on with their relations, who had their own wagon and horses but, to Dieter's consternation, "her horses were so little, they looked like seaside ponies".

After travelling slowly along quiet country roads as daylight faded to snow-lit night, the group stopped at a big farm.

"Our relative decided then that her horses weren't strong enough to pull us all, so we were alone," said Dieter.

However fate intervened yet again in the sudden appearance of his uncle, Otto Neumann, Aunt Herta's husband, now in charge of a local section of the people's militia.

"That was our great blessing," said Dieter. "He was staying there too, with a group of men and half-a-dozen wagons, all in retreat."

Relieved to be sleeping in a warm cowshed crowded with refugees, Dieter thankfully drank the early morning milk garnered by his mother as stories of the Russian encirclement flew all around him.

It was the night among so many nights sheltering in strange places which four-year-old Doris would remember all her life.

"We slept with many others in the aisle of the cow barn but we were lucky because Uncle Otto, as part of the Volksturm, had access to food. That was to stand us in good stead as the worst was yet to come."

It was decided that the family would head off to Frische Haff with Otto in his wagon. Before they left, travelling through the night, the ever-resourceful Otto had screws added to the horses' hooves to prevent them sliding on the ice.

By eleven o'clock the next morning, the family was gazing across the lagoon's icy stretch which, for Dieter at least, held an unlikely touch of magic.

"It looked wonderful. The sun was shining and the ice glistened. A German soldier told me it was about thirty centimetres thick."

Among the hordes of people crossing the ice was another schoolboy, eleven-year-old farmer's son Erhard Schulz. Like Dieter, he had been brusquely uprooted from his childhood home, a farm just south of the River Memel.

In his memoir, "Farewell to East Prussia", Schulz describes how his family, too, had been forced to change direction, heading for Frische Haff as the Russians closed in.

He recalled: "Before us extended an infinite plane of ice. It seemed endless in every direction. The horizon wasn't clearly visible because of the distant haze…there was nothing but ice."

Hurriedly sheltering with his mother under the family's wagon as Russian planes attacked from above, he heard "a buzzing, as if pieces of ice or iron splinters were flying through the air".

Surprised to find himself recalling the words of the Lord's Prayer he had learned as a young child, he saw that "fountains of ice and water were splashing up to our right. The ice was tilting up and down, as if a wave was moving underneath".

Schulz and his family survived but, writing years later, he said: "I believe this experience threw me back in my development by several years. I receded into my dream world and recalled the days of my peaceful, carefree childhood."

Dieter, too, was all too aware of the dangers they faced.

"On our way to the Frische Haff I had looked down from the wagon and seen dead bodies. They seemed to be Russians, which showed there had been fighting there. But I knew there was no way out of East Prussia except over the ice."

The family joined a long line of wagons moving slowly forward under the direction of the army.

"We were told to keep a distance of about thirty metres between the wagons to stop the ice from cracking, but by that evening things had changed and there were two or three lines, all heading in the same direction."

As the day wore on and more and more desperate people joined the exodus across the lagoon, the ice, inevitably, began to give way in places. Tramping slowly through the water pooling on the surface of the sinking ice, hoping against hope that the wagon alongside her where her children sheltered would not disappear through the melting ice, Erna saw sights she would never forget.

For even as the ice itself began to break up, she and her fellow refugees, like the Schulz family, were always in danger of attack from the Russian planes circling overhead.

It was, as one Russian pilot admitted many years later, "impossible to miss" the straggling lines of people and wagons moving so slowly across the bomb-riddled ice beneath them. Without camouflage or shelter, they were sitting targets.

Rosemarie Miles Apsel, whose 1967 memoir, "Last Minute: Our Escape from East Prussia", includes a description of the refugees "on foot, on sled, wagon, skis, bicycle or on horseback", saw "huge holes in the ice" where bombs had fallen.

She wrote: "The crowd panicked. In desperate attempts to overcome the obstacle they hurriedly broke up wagons and placed loose boards across the wide craters, pushing and shoving, and people, vehicles and horses fell into the icy waters."

According to the writer's mother, one woman who made it to the other side sat on the ice with slashed wrists - all five of her children had drowned.

Another rushed back across the ice in search of a missing child, only to find that, wrapped in blankets and numb from cold, it had slid silently off the back of a sled without anyone noticing.

For Erna, a particularly vivid memory would be of horses' heads, the only part still visible as they and their cargo disappeared through the ice.

Talking to her younger son, Peter, years later, she said: "They looked awful, their eyes were white and bulging."

Dieter recalled: "It was dreadful. There was a lot of standing still because it was so congested, it meant people couldn't get onto the land on the spit easily."

In these dire circumstances, as temperatures dropped to minus twenty degrees, a journey which had taken earlier escapees just four hours lasted thirty hours as day turned to night and back to day again.

"In war, everything changes dramatically all the time," said Dieter. "In the distance I saw where a wagon had dropped into the ice, and I saw a young chap ice skating with a little boat and a sail. He was going very fast and I thought: 'He can go all the way to the west like that!'"

Straining his eyes on the land ahead as the light faded, he could see sand dunes and the occasional plume of smoke.

"I knew someone was cooking their evening meal."

Finally scrambling onto the two-kilometre wide spit of land - Frische Nehrung - on the far side of the lagoon at the end of their second day on the ice, the family was caught up in another slow-moving line picking its way through a road full of potholes.

For Rosemarie Miles Apsel, whose family had had a summer house there before the war, this area between the lagoon and "the beautiful, gentle, sunny Baltic Sea" had been a place of enchantment.

But on that winter's day in 1945, the dreaming pine forests and quiet sandy beaches stretching away in both directions had been turned into a nightmarish hell on earth.

"I saw people with feet swollen and full of blisters," said Dieter. "They had walked over the ice, probably pushing a sled or a pram. I couldn't believe it, it made me so mad. I felt so sorry for them - they were human beings, after all."

Turning off the crowded road into a small clearing under the trees, the family rested briefly while Otto set about lighting a fire.

However Dieter, taking the first longed-for mouthful of pea soup hastily made in a big metal jam container, was not impressed.

"At home, my mother made it with smoked bacon, but the piece we brought with us had nearly all gone by then, so my uncle's soup didn't taste the same."

As they rejoined the trek, Erna, desperate to change baby Hanne-Lore's cold and soaking nappy, knocked on the door of a nearby house, only to be turned away because it was already full.

Once again, Uncle Otto came to the rescue.

"He banged on the door and said: 'You must let this lady in, she has a baby in her arms who needs seeing to'," recalled Dieter.

Relenting, the woman allowed mother and baby inside, and the rest of the family spent that night wrapped in furs in their wagon.

"We felt safe now, on this spit of land, and warm. I will never forget that day - it was my tenth birthday, February 16, 1945," recalled Dieter.

Looking back towards his homeland as he and his family travelled slowly along the spit through the "ghostly, dim light of the night", Erhard Schulz watched the "strangely glowing sky in the east...the sky on fire stretching from the north to the south".

He recalled: "The whole of East Prussia seemed to be a single fire blaze. A permanent low rumbling and thundering was to be heard."

After their perilous journey, the Teubler family was within two days of Danzig, from where ships taking part in "Operation Hannibal", one of the largest emergency evacuations by sea in history, were ferrying refugees and soldiers to safety. By the war's end in May, up to 900,000 civilians and 350,000 soldiers would have been carried across the Baltic to western Germany or Denmark.

However not everyone made it. Just two weeks before, one of the deadliest maritime disasters in history had ended the lives of thousands of men, women and children.

Late on the evening of January 30, transport ship the Wilhelm Gustloff, a former Nazi luxury cruise liner crammed with over ten thousand passengers, sank in just forty-five minutes after being hit by three Soviet torpedoes. With little protection, it had been heading across the open sea towards Kiel. Only some 1,200 survived the deadly attack.

Less than two weeks later, the SS General von Steuben met a similar fate, Soviet torpedoes wiping out almost all the 2,680 refugees on board.

On the road to Danzig - icy, flat and bitterly cold - Dieter's attention was caught by mysterious packages tied to every tree along the route.

He recalled: "I discovered they were explosives, put there so that the road could be blocked by fallen trees."

The country boy was also fascinated to note the doorbells outside every house, a formality quite unknown in rural Memelland.

Finally arriving in Danzig Lang Fur (now Wrzeszcz, in Poland), a well-to-do suburb some four miles from the city centre, Dieter watched from the wagon as SS stormtroopers surged among the waves of people moving through to grab more men and boys for Hitler's Volkssturm.

It was then that he and his family were overjoyed to catch sight of his father, Franz, clad in his army uniform, directing traffic.

"It was a great thing for us. He had heard we were on our way so he was looking out for us, and he directed us away from the other wagons."

One of Franz's tasks was to confiscate tents from people on the trek for use by the military.

Doris recalled: "He hated doing it but that's how the German military worked: never mind civilians, it was more important to keep the soldiers dry."

Her mother agreed, later commenting with a shrug: "It was wartime."

The short stay in Danzig provided much-needed rest after the tension of the long trek.

"They found us a very nice apartment, almost elegant, in Lang Fur," said Dieter. "We stayed about a week and we ate well and recovered."

To Erna's relief, her sister, Herta, and her children also arrived safely.

"But they just missed Uncle Otto because he had reported for duty with his horses and wagons earlier that same day," said Dieter.

Deciding that escape by sea was still the best option, Erna did her best to secure places for her family on one of the ships sailing from Danzig ports. However the queues were growing longer by the day as exhausted refugees arrived, so in the end they had to rely on Franz to find a way for them to travel overland.

"After a few days, he managed to arrange for us to be transported to Stolp (now Slupsk,in Poland), about eighty miles away, in a military wagon," said Dieter.

But first, in case any of her children became lost or separated from the family, the ever-practical Erna made each of them labels to hang around their necks giving their name, age and place of birth.

Finally arriving in Stolp, a handsome old city on the border of the former Polish corridor, the family found themselves in a place gripped by fear. In January, some fifty thousand prisoners from nearby Stutthof concentration camp had been forced to march out across the frozen landscape towards the west as the defeated Nazis tried to remove evidence of their crimes. They left behind around eight hundred murdered in the railway yard at Stolp station.

But it was the advancing Russian army, reportedly just days away, which was spreading panic through the population. Erna knew she had to keep moving, and immediately went to the Red Cross to ask for help.

"She didn't get anywhere," recalled Dieter. "They said there were no trains going west 'at the moment'. That was the way it was at that time, you never knew what would happen next."

Desperate to find a way of moving her young family on, however, Erna had the good fortune to bump into an old schoolmate from her home town. A train driver, he was about to haul a dozen locomotives west to prevent them from falling into Russian hands.

"He said he had room for two passengers, but my mother persuaded him to take all six of us," said Dieter.

Their departure was not a moment too soon. The Red Army would reach Stolp on March 8, their threatened arrival reputedly driving around a thousand inhabitants of the old city to commit suicide rather than face the well-reported fury of soldiers bent on revenge. By the time they left, Stolp's historic centre would be all but wiped out.

But, while the train had offered a vital means of escape from the terrified city, the journey would prove almost fatal for Dieter's younger brother. With no heating and frequent stops to give way to military and medical trains, nine-year-old Peter, still weak from a bout of scarlet fever as a young child, grew steadily weaker.

"He was ill, he looked so pale and yellow we thought he was dying," said Dieter. "After travelling almost three hundred kilometres, my mother decided we couldn't stay on the locomotive, it was just too cold, so she got us all out at Pasewalk."

As the family hauled their bags through the streets of the old town where Adolf Hitler, wounded by a gas attack, had been treated at the end of the First World War, Erna searched, as usual, for somewhere to shelter for the night.

Tired and hungry, four-year-old Doris wailed: "I can't walk any more."

Eventually, spotting a deserted dress shop, Erna shepherded her family inside and they huddled together for warmth through the long night.

The next morning, knowing the Red Cross was still operating in many towns, the ever-resourceful Erna sought them out and asked for help. This time she struck lucky. The organisation was putting together a train to move refugees away from Pasewalk and she and her children were offered seats.

Two months later, the town would be overrun by the Red Army.

Before they left, Erna sent word to her husband, who was still in Danzig, to let him know their whereabouts.

"Incredibly, the post still worked at that time," said Dieter. "We told him we were headed for Saxony."

However, as happened so often in these uncertain times, the packed train moved not into western Germany but north-west, following the line of the Baltic coast into Schleswig Holstein, Germany's most northerly province. For, unbeknown to Erna, Saxony's ancient capital city, Dresden, had been devastated by three days of Allied bombing. The firestorm which followed had killed thousands of people and left the city in smoking ruins.

At the end of a 360 kilometre rail journey lasting several days, the family found themselves in the small riverside town of Preetz.

"By now, everyone knew the war was lost," said Dieter. "We were given places in an army barracks. It was pretty run down and almost deserted because most of the soldiers had been sent to the front. There were air raid sirens going all the time, short bursts for warning then a long note for the all-clear."

However what mattered most to the hungry family after their long journey was the appearance of generous supplies of army sandwiches.

"They were lovely," recalled Dieter.

It was here, knowing a return to their old life was impossible, at least for the foreseeable future, that Erna was forced to draw breath and take a decision which she knew would shape her family's future.

"There was a choice of various places to go from there, but one of the army officers collecting our names told my mother we should go to Laboe," recalled Dieter. "He said it would be good with little children because it was a seaside holiday place."

And so, following what seemed a logical piece of advice, the family picked up their bags yet again to set out on the final stage of a four-month journey which had tested them all to the very limits of endurance.

For Erna, just thirty years old, a young wife and mother who had lived her whole life in a rural backwater surrounded by friends and family, the trek had brought unimaginable challenges. Responsible for four young children and her teenage stepdaughter, constantly seeking food and shelter, she had been forced to rely on luck and the kindness of others in order to survive.

Dieter, always conscious that he must take his father's role as best he could, and keenly aware of the need to move swiftly, would recall that sense of anxiety throughout his life.

But even as they travelled towards their final destination, first the short journey to the heavily-bombed port of Kiel and then up through the Kiel Fjord to Laboe, on the shores of the Baltic Sea, the young family felt danger all around.

In the months since the autumn day when they left their home for the last time, the Allies had drastically stepped up their bombing campaign in Germany, leaving a trail of devastation right across the country. Cities, towns and even out-of-the-way factories had been pummelled day and night for months, and the recent attack on Dresden had been carried out by no less than 1250 British and American planes dropping almost four thousand tons of bombs and incendiary devices onto the city.

Kiel itself, a major naval base and home of Germany's feared U-boats - dubbed the "Wolf Pack" - which inflicted so much damage on Allied ships, had been a major target throughout the conflict, leaving much of the town destroyed. The city also found itself on the enemy flight paths to major cities like Hamburg and Berlin, triggering the frequent boom of raid warnings which added to the fear and anxiety.

"We were all very nervous of mines and bombardment," said Dieter, recalling the final stages of their long journey.

However they arrived safely in Laboe, and were pleasantly surprised to be met on the quayside by a schoolboy waiting to carry their luggage in a handcart.

"He took us to a restaurant where we had traditional thick pea soup with ham organised by the Red Cross," said Dieter, still relishing that comforting taste of home.

The date was March 3, 1945. It would be another two months until the war ended and the daily fear of attack was always there, but at last Erna and her children could begin to make a new life in the little town which would be their home for almost a decade.

Franz and Erna's wedding in 1933

Newly-weds Erna and Franz with Werner and Hilla, the children from his first marriage.

Otto Neumann and his family lived well in the prewar years.

Erna (right) in the garden at Nattkischken in the early war years.

Erna with Essen refugee Frau Joswig.

Franz and Erna with Doris outside the wartime Red Cross station based at the family farm.

Hitler's triumphant entry into Memel in 1939.

National Digital Archives, Poland.

The last family Christmas before the death of oldest son Werner in a freak wartime accident.

Werner Teubler (left) with a naval colleague.

East Prussians flee from the invading Red Army.

akg-images-ullstein bild.

Refugees arriving in Schleswig Holstein in 1945.

bundesarchiv.

The family found refuge in first floor rooms in Haus Katzbek in Laboe.

Laboe had been a popular seaside resort since Edwardian times.

Dieter (left) with his mother and siblings in the garden at Haus Katzbek.

Doris (right), with sister Hanne-Lore, found school life in Laboe a daily struggle.

Franz Teubler kept chickens, rabbits and pigs in a field alongside Haus Katzbek.

Confirmation in 1950.

Dieter (right) with his family in Laboe.

Essen in 1954 was still recovering from heavy wartime bombing.

An early holiday in Austria.

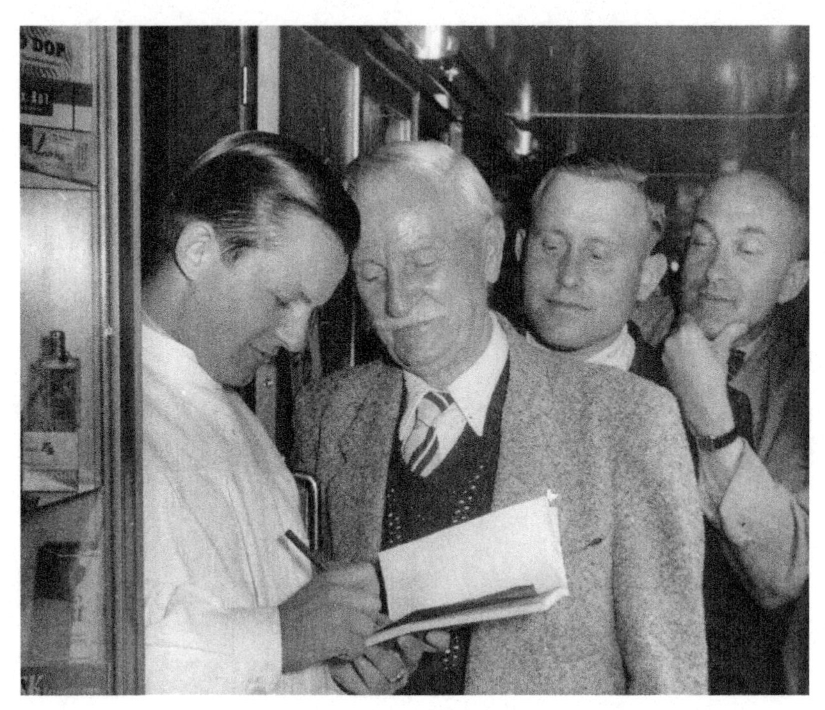

Checking in clients on the popular Touropa Express.

Erna and Fritz Streve celebrate their wedding with her children.

Susan Waters played at Wimbledon for seven years.

Susan Teubler with her parents, Alfred and Sybil Waters.

Dieter and Susan were married in December 1960.

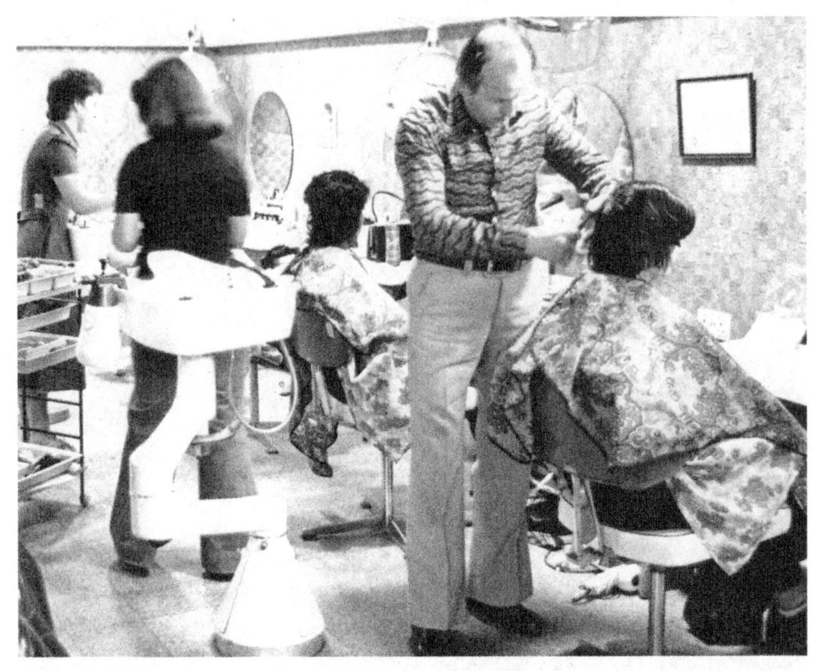

Dieter imported modern German equipment for his first salon, in Hawkhurst near Tunbridge Wells.

The Dieter Henry salon in Hawkhurst.

Dieter and Susan with their four children.

Dieter instructs hairdressing students at a local college.

Dieter and his step-sister, Hilla, first returned to the old family farm, now home to Lithuanian families, in 1991.

Dieter with his family beside the memorial erected on the site of the old village church in Nattkischken.

Chapter 4.

A NEW LIFE BEGINS

"I undid the string, and inside was a revolver with six bullets. I immediately understood: my father had loaded one for each of us in case the worst happened. I closed it up again and threw it into the pond."

Carrying their few possessions, still in the same clothes they had worn when they left their farm in Memelland five months earlier, Dieter and his family set forth from the restaurant on the final stage of their journey.

Walking up Katzbek, one of the streets sloping up from the waterfront, they caught their first glimpse of Haus Katzbek, outlined against the sky at the top.

The solid early twentieth century house which was to be their home for the next seven years was set in well-tended grounds at the end of a curving drive. It was owned by Hermann Wulff, a former town mayor, and his wife, Elisabeth. Comfortably settled into retirement, enjoying their pretty garden and regular musical gatherings around the piano in their elegant salon, the couple were less than pleased by the arrival of the dishevelled family.

"They seemed to have no idea of the suffering the war had brought," said Dieter who, hustled unceremoniously up the stairs by their host as his family watched below, realised early on that they were not welcome.

He said: "The maid, Anna, lived at the top of the house. We were allocated three rooms on the first floor alongside a lady called Frau Busse. We had a living room leading into the kitchen, where Peter and I slept, and a bedroom next door along the landing where my mother and the girls slept."

But despite the rather frigid atmosphere, Haus Katzbek offered Erna and her children a sense of security they had not felt since leaving their home the previous autumn.

"We had nothing when we arrived, only what we could carry," said Dieter. "But people gave us garden chairs to sit on, and we had a kind of cupboard, just four uprights covered with a bedspread -we called it 'the body cupboard' because it looked like a standing coffin. My mother cooked for us all on a single ring - Frau Busse had a lovely big cooker, but although she let my mother use it at first, she soon changed her mind. After all, we were five children."

Soon after they arrived in Laboe, Dieter's mother took him aside and handed him a small package neatly parcelled up with string, instructing him to throw it into a nearby pond. It was then that he made a chilling discovery.

"Of course, I wanted to know what it was," said Dieter. "I undid the string, and inside was a revolver with six bullets. I immediately understood: my father had loaded one for each of us in case the worst happened. I closed it up again and threw it into the pond."

With a little money still left, and the hope that they would eventually be able to return to Nattkischken still lingering, the family began slowly to recover from their painful journey.

"It was very nice at first," said Dieter. "We had heard nothing from our father and we didn't know where the rest of the family were either, but we were so happy to be safe and we knew the war would end soon. There were still air raid sirens going off - we had to go down to the cellar with our hosts - but it was relatively peaceful, and there were so many people in the same boat."

However the sheer number of refugees pouring into Laboe soon began to put a strain on the local population. As a popular holiday resort, it had offered welcome income to local people letting out rooms during the summer and, when the tourists had gone, its inhabitants were used to enjoying the quieter winter months. But as more and more refugees poured in, the population first doubled, then trebled and, as the weeks passed, grew out of all proportion to the size of the little town.

Apart from the crowds of people, which gave rise to some hostility, there was also a sense of otherness about the newcomers from distant East Prussia which made life uncomfortable for everyone.

For, as Patricia Clough suggests in her book, The Flight Across the Ice: "Local inhabitants, struggling with their own losses and suffering, did not want to know about, or simply did not believe, the far more terrible experiences of the East Prussians. They often assumed that the haggard, unkempt, often ragged people arriving on the treks had always lived like that, that they were vagabonds and inferior beings, and they treated them accordingly."

She added: "Some told East Prussians that their problems were their own fault, that they should have stayed at home and made the best of life under the Russians."

For Dieter, however, ever willing to seek out the best in human nature, "It was understandable. Laboe had been a small, quiet town before the war. It was hard for the local people, but some were very kind to us".

Just two months after their arrival, as the family began to settle into their new seaside home, Dieter awoke to a sound which he would remember all his life. It was the noise of guns going off, shooting which would continue throughout the day, along with the swoosh of rockets arcing through the summer sky.

The date was May 8, 1945. Guessing immediately what all this activity meant, Dieter hurried to his mother and said: "I think the war is over."

The news was soon confirmed on the radio.

"All that day, people were getting rid of the ammunition they had stored. It was all blown up," said Dieter. "We were so relieved that the pressure of war had gone. We finally had our freedom."

However he, like everyone else, realised there were enormous challenges still to come.

"Germany was absolutely down. All the cities - Cologne, Hamburg, Dusseldorf, Berlin - they were all destroyed, some as much as eighty per cent, all just rubble."

There were also an estimated two million displaced people wandering across Europe - concentration camp survivors and German civilians rushing west to escape the Red Army along with the remnants of Hitler's defeated troops, which included Ukrainians, Italians and Hungarians.

The Allies now in power, plans made by leaders Winston Churchill, Franklin D Roosevelt and Joseph Stalin for the break-up and occupation of Nazi Germany by foreign powers went ahead. And in the new, postwar Europe, Memelland, along with the whole of East Prussia, would simply disappear.

Under pressure from Stalin, a new German/Polish border following the Oder and Neisse rivers southwards from Swinoujscie on the Baltic Sea right down to the borders of Czechoslovakia was agreed. Land to the east - including major Prussian cities like Danzig, Königsberg, Breslau (now Wroclaw, in Poland) and Stettin (now Szczecin, in Poland) - all came under Soviet occupation. Memelland, which Hitler had brought back to Germany just six years earlier, would return to Lithuania.

But despite the dizzying changes taking place across Europe, refugees like the Teublers still clung tenaciously to the dream of returning home.

"In those first months, there was still hope," said Dieter.

However the mass expulsions of Germans from the eastern territories in the months to come would destroy the last vestige of that dream of home. According to recent research, over twelve million Germans either fled during the war or were forcibly evacuated later. By 1950, the number of ethnic Germans living in Central and Eastern Europe would be just twelve per cent of the prewar total.

But for the moment, largely unaware of events outside, the struggle to survive from day-to-day was paramount in Erna's mind.

"We were just so poor," said Dieter. "We were always hungry, always thinking about food, especially when delicious smells from the Wulffs' kitchen downstairs floated up."

Scolded for picking redcurrants and gooseberries growing in the garden, Dieter and his brother made sure birds did not steal the cherries growing in the next door field by feeding a long dangling string from their bedroom window to scare them off.

"Hunger made us very inventive, you developed a wider perspective. All kinds of things went on. We all needed shoes, but you could only get them by bargaining, usually with food. Our beds were made of straw, so we had to ask the farmers for fresh straw when it became too broken up. We needed it for our pigs and chickens too, but we knew they were short themselves so we always pretended it was for our own beds."

Their desperate situation was mirrored throughout the shattered country.

By 1947, food production per head had halved since 1938 and industrial output was down by two-thirds. However the Allies had agreed between themselves that no German should have more food than those whose countries had been occupied by Hitler during the long war years. No relief supplies were allowed into Germany and imports were forbidden, at least in the early months. But while the Teublers' situation in Laboe was bad, in the big cities it was even worse.

In his 1955 book, Mainsprings of the German Revival (1955), Henry Wallich wrote: "Each day, and particularly on weekends, vast hordes of people trekked out to the country to barter food from the farmers. In dilapidated railway carriages from which everything pilferable had long disappeared, on the roofs and on the running boards, hungry people travelled sometimes hundreds of miles at snail's pace to where they hoped to find something to eat. They took their wares - personal effects, old clothes, sticks of furniture, whatever bombed-out remnants they had - and came back with grain or potatoes for a week or two."

In Krupp's famous locomotive works in Essen, the day ended at 3.30pm to enable workers to go out of the city to look for food. A contemporary British report noted: "It is usual in the late afternoon to find strings of bicycles carrying sacks of vegetables and stretching many miles along the roads leading to the larger towns."

Hanne-Lore, by now beginning to see beyond the world of early childhood, recalled: "One day, mother went to Berlin with a bucketful of herrings, very tightly packed in layers of salt. She brought back alcohol, vodka and so on to swap for food."

In order to reach Berlin, some three hundred kilometres away, Erna had to cross from West Germany to communist East Germany across the so-called "Green Border", at this time relatively easy to do. As more and more East Germans poured out of their Soviet-occupied country, however, the heavily-guarded border would become a potent symbol of what Winston Churchill dubbed the "Iron Curtain".

Yearning for a bicycle, Dieter was delighted one day to come across a discarded bike frame and, after much searching, he eventually found two wheels. They had no tyres but, convinced he could make it work, he scavenged a long piece of rubber from the beach.

"I took it home and it fitted beautifully around the wheels. I made little holes and bound it on, then fitted ballbearings all around."

After bumping triumphantly along for just a few metres, however, Dieter finally had to acknowledge that even his considerable powers of invention were beaten when all the ballbearings clattered to the ground.

"I just had to wait until I could buy something better."

Following the postwar division of Nazi Germany into Allied occupation zones, the sight of groups of British soldiers in the streets of Laboe had become commonplace.

"I remember crouching in the bushes to watch the British tanks rolling down past our house into the town," said Dieter. "We didn't know what they would look like, but they were very decent and friendly."

The "Tommies" walking along the promenade also gave Dieter and his brother an unexpected opportunity to earn a little money.

"We would walk thirty metres behind them and pick up their dropped cigarette ends so that we could take out the tobacco to sell or exchange," said Dieter. "When they began to realise what we were doing, some of them would throw away half a cigarette. They probably felt sorry for us."

Life at the boys' new school in Laboe brought fresh trials, made harder for Dieter by his undiagnosed dyslexia. Local children laughed at his regional accent and, recalling his struggle one day to decipher particular letters, he said: "The class thought I was stupid and the teacher nearly went berserk."

Clothes provided by an aunt living far away in America only underlined the boys' difference.

He said: "Our great aunt, Klara Bruning, one of our grandmother's sisters, lived in America, in Pasadena. In 1946, my mother wrote to her and said we'd lost everything. She began to send us regular care parcels which were wonderful to receive, I jumped high for joy when they came. At first it was food - tins, dried eggs and so on - but later Peter and I got knickerbockers and bright red pullovers. We were the most outstandingly dressed people in the class."

But while new clothes were welcome, for the two boys their eyecatching attire proved "rather embarrassing", admitted Dieter. "We were teased like hell, the children sang a rude song whenever we passed."

With fond memories of games of table tennis in their Uncle Otto's house in Nattkischken, Dieter and his brother were thrilled when they heard that evening table tennis sessions were to be held in the school gym hall. Arriving full of anticipation, however, they were deeply upset to be turned away because they did not have the right shoes.

"We felt very sad," said Dieter.

But while he enjoyed sports lessons and playground games, he and Peter agreed that bunking off school to go out into the fields or kill rabbits was much more fun.

"We worked for local farmers and we also used to collect coal lying in the road for heating our house."

On one never-to-be-forgotten day, Dieter came across something which his younger sister, Doris, would remember all her life.

Catching sight of what looked like an old sack lying in the road, he "had a feeling there was some kind of food in it, and my goodness, there was! There was a chicken and a dozen eggs and sausage. Thank God! We didn't know who it belonged to, so it was ours! We had a feast, it was lovely."

Doris agreed, recalling: "Dieter finding that sack was like three Christmases in one!"

Spotted by a neighbour as they enjoyed the rare treat, Erna quickly made up a story about the food being sent by relatives.

"You were supposed to notify the authorities if you found anything like that," explained Dieter.

Soon after they arrived, Hilla's fiancé, Walter, managed to track them down and the young couple, forced apart, like so many others, by the war, wasted no time in arranging their wedding.

"Frau Busse let them use her sitting room for a little reception, just tea and cakes," said Dieter, still faintly resentful that children were not invited.

The couple settled in a flat on the seafront, and Walter, more accustomed to farming than shop-keeping, supported them by selling icecream and confectionery from a hut on the beach. Their first child, Hans Werner - named for his mother's lost brother - was born in 1946. Four years later, their daughter, Gabriela, was born.

Adapting to his new life, Walter proved an astute tradesman, eventually opening a small grocery shop some one hundred kilometres away in Suderstapel, which he successfully converted into a pioneering self-service outlet.

News of Erna's mother, Ella, finally arrived via a notification from the Red Cross to pick her up in Cologne.

"She and our grandfather had got separated and she ended up staying on a farm," said Dieter, who went with his mother to collect her the next day.

His grandfather also arrived in Laboe, this time via Lübeck. Frail and ill with dysentery and heart problems, he died soon afterwards.

"I remember seeing his body being carried out of our house," said Dieter, who had been close to his grandfather. "His feet were sticking out from under the cover, and I noticed my grandmother had put on a pair of new socks."

Hanne-Lore also remembered that day, "standing with my grandmother at the end of the bed in silent prayer".

In 1947, when the family had been in Laboe for some two years, a ring on the doorbell brought a welcome surprise.

"I opened the door and there was my father," said Dieter. "He told us he had been in a prisoner-of-war camp in Russia for some months, working as a cook. Then later he stayed with his sister, Frieda, five hundred kilometres away from Laboe in Thuringia, in East Germany. He didn't find out where we were for a while, even though we had sent our address to a relative in Berlin."

His appearance was a welcome relief to his son, now twelve years old, for so long acutely aware of his role as "the man of the family". For while children from farming families had always been part of the farm economy, whether helping to care for the animals or working in the fields, Dieter's wartime responsibilities had weighed heavily.

He said: "There was one night I remember when I would go to sleep then start dreaming, having nightmares about the Russians coming. We had been told so many different things about what the Russians did. It was about ten o'clock, the adults were still up, talking, and I just grabbed my pillow and ran."

Once back with his family, Franz lost no time in looking for ways to support them.

"He found a job working for farmers, but at haymaking time he was suffering badly from asthma up in the hayloft, so he asked his employer if he could be moved," said Dieter.

Accused of simply being lazy, the proud man, who for years had been a successful businessman and community leader, threw down his tools on the spot and walked away.

His next job was in Kiel harbour, where he was in charge of lifting submarines out of the water for disposal by the Allies, who had taken possession of all Germany's deadly U-boats at the end of the war.

It was a job which proved to have unexpected advantages.

"He found tins and tins of cheese, which was great," said Dieter. "But he also brought home leather jackets and trousers worn by the U-boat crews. My mother sent them to a tailor to be made into lederhosen and so on."

Years later, Erna would laugh to recall how, worried that her sons would be beaten for failing to do their homework, she had hit on the idea of stuffing newspapers into the seats of their leather trousers to dull the pain.

Among the family's more thoughtful neighbours was Hans Otto Wulff, a gentleman farmer whose old redbrick farmhouse was just across the road from Haus Katzbeck.

"He was a very good man. He let my father use the field by our house to keep chickens and rabbits, and two pigs which provided us with ham and sausages."

Nearby was another member of the extended Wulff family.

"Otto Wulff was also a farmer, as well as a very powerful figure in the area. He was a county administrator responsible for settling land disputes and so on," said Dieter.

"Peter and I used to help gather potatoes on his farm, too. He paid us in potatoes, and after the harvest we were allowed to go and pick up leftovers. We worked so fast one season that we managed to gather seven hundred pounds!"

With up to thirty rabbits to feed, the boys were also sent out to find food for them.

"We were not allowed to pick from the fields, so we had to fill our sacks from the roadside," said Dieter, who would watch as his mother steamed the precious meat and stored it in sealed jars for the barren winter months.

The boys also made peat bricks out of turf, cut into neat briquettes and carefully dried before being used for heating and cooking. Another task was to collect wood as his father set out to build a shed and pens for the animals.

Once settled, Franz quickly made useful local connections with other refugees from East Prussia.

"He had saved four iron wheels from Kiel harbour, and after a local blacksmith had made a wagon base, an East Prussian craftsman built the platform."

Meanwhile, with her mother now in charge of the household, Erna had set up a small shop overlooking the harbour in Laboe selling wool and woollen clothes. She also repaired laddered nylon stockings using a small hook, painstaking work which proved popular with local women in these difficult times.

"My mother always resented the fact that she had not been allowed to work or learn a trade," said Dieter. "Her family was reasonably well off, so she had had private tutors, but the idea was that she would marry, which she did. But she was very good at making clothes, she had a good eye, and she was ambitious, she always had the idea that in business you could make lots of money."

However lack of cash to buy stock always held Erna back which is why, despite the fact that Dieter and his brother had worked long hours for local farmers to save money for a much-anticipated school trip, she took it for her business.

"She was very much her own person, not always an easy mix," said Dieter.

He recalled: "Grandmother stayed with us for a number of years. She was always in the kitchen cooking and she slept with the girls. She got very crochety sometimes, and we would have to sit on her back and massage it. I didn't like that, but it was what it was."

As the strict food restrictions gradually loosened, the desperate hunger pangs suffered by Dieter and his siblings were somewhat eased by regular school meals supplied by the British Army.

"There was a huge military cooker in the school where they cooked dried beans and other food sent from America," said Dieter. "We took metal containers to school and they would fill them up with soup. It was quite nice, and you'd sometimes get someone else's portion if they didn't like it - the local children were not as hungry as us."

On one red-letter day, each child was provided with two bars of chocolate by the Government.

"I swapped one of mine for ten eggs for the family," said Dieter

The family also took on a nearby allotment so that they could grow their own fruit and vegetables.

But while their brothers knew all too well what they had left behind, for younger sisters Doris and Hanne-Lore, just four and two when they arrived, life in Laboe was almost all they had ever known.

For Doris, however, a quiet, rather pensive child, haunting images of their journey across Europe would remain.

"I remembered standing by the wagon with my coat on the day we were told we could finally leave Memelland. And on the trek, I recalled staying overnight in a big barn, with cows on either side of us. We had to do quite a lot of walking. We were suffering, I was always saying, 'I've got a fever'. There is so much you can't remember, but it is probably within you."

More aware of her surroundings than her younger sister, Doris, like Dieter, sensed some hostility in Laboe.

"I think unconsciously I absorbed a lot. The Wulffs had been forced to take us in. They were in their eighties, they didn't want us and they were not generous. They wouldn't share their bread with us and it was hard to smell bacon frying when we were often under-nourished."

She added: "Laboe was in an agrarian landscape where people had lived for centuries. It was overrun with refugees and there was such strong pressure to accommodate them in any little place. A lot ended up in big barns divided into sections."

Starting school in Laboe, Doris quickly became unhappy and withdrawn.

Recalling the old school buildings filled to overflowing with the influx of refugee children, she said: "People were ignorant, there was a lack of education and they were often hostile. I had no friends. The local children didn't want to know, they made our lives difficult."

Sitting silently at the back of the class, the small girl took no part in lessons during her early school years. On a day she would remember all her life, the teacher put her in front of the class and told them: "Doris is stupid."

In fact, she was simply very short-sighted, but it would be a number of years before it was recognised and her natural intelligence allowed to blossom. In the meantime, like refugees all over Germany, she suffered.

For Hanne-Lore, however, life was more straightforward.

"One of my earliest memories was of a vehicle full of soldiers after our wagon crashed. My sister was given biscuits and I was not, that is what I remember mainly. But I had no sense of fear because I was so young, and I don't remember arriving in Laboe."

More outgoing than her older sister, Hanne-Lore was growing into an energetic, rather fearless child who could outrun her brothers, loved speeding along on any bicycle she could find and yearned for a sledge of her own, a luxury beyond her family's means. Walking alone to meet her sister from school one freezing winter's day, she had to be rescued by a woman who saw her fall through the ice on a local pond as she set out to slide across it.

Remembering with pride the dark blue winter coats fashioned by their mother from an old dyed blanket, complete with hoods lined in red, she said: "My father also made us wooden stools for sitting round the kitchen table - the smallest, which I still have, was for me."

For both girls, however, the lush garden and nearby fields surrounding their new home offered hours of pleasure and, recalled Doris: "We often walked down the road to the sandy beaches of the fjord, where the water was shallow enough to paddle safely."

In 1950, aged fifteen, Dieter left school to find his way in a world where opportunities were few.

He recalled: "Most of us left at that age, although some went on to university. But I wasn't university material and anyway, my family had no money, we were still just surviving."

With hopes of training to be an electrician quickly dashed, Dieter reluctantly agreed to taking on a hairdressing apprenticeship arranged by his father.

"I wasn't very happy, it was very boring, but I knew there were no other jobs going in Laboe. It was a sad period in my life, I was very depressed - after all, I was aiming to be a millionaire!"

Shortly after his fifteenth birthday, at Easter 1950, Dieter was confirmed, always an important event for which relations would gather and celebration cakes would be baked. However a photograph taken that day captures the uncharacteristic sense of despair felt by the teenager, smart in a suit and tie. He recalled: "The future looked pretty black."

As the weeks passed, his depression only increased.

"After spending six months learning to lather our male clients, I was at last allowed to handle a real cut-throat razor to practise. Not on clients at first, of course, but on a lathered balloon. Making a mistake meant a burst balloon and shaving foam everywhere."

One of two young apprentices being trained by salon owner Reinhold Noetsel and his wife, a stylist, Dieter was earning very little.

"I remember an old schoolfriend came in one day and told me he was earning two hundred deutsche marks a month as a mattress maker. I was only earning twenty-five, which my mother kept because it was needed by the family. I thought about leaving, but I always came back to thinking that in three years I'd be qualified."

What made matters much worse was the knowledge that his strong, energetic father, a potent role model throughout his life, was dying. Franz Teubler was suffering from cancer, and in November 1950 he died, aged fifty-seven.

However advice he gave Dieter during his final days would help his grieving son through those first sad months.

"He had been a very successful businessman, and he told me that if I wanted to make myself independent, I must remember that I could easily equip myself for practically nothing, just a mirror, comb and scissors."

Looking back on "times when I felt I wasn't making great progress because I had to learn quite a few things", Dieter said: "Then I found it helpful to go to my father's grave and talk to him in my head."

Now almost ten years old, Doris was also aware that her father was dying.

She said: "I remember him in hospital and during his last few weeks at home. He was very poorly, often screaming in great pain."

Having seen little of her father as a young child, to his older daughter he was a slightly distant figure.

"But I often think of him, and I do remember a day when, after a visit to a hospital, he took me to a milk bar in Kiel. He bought me a glass of milk and we sat there together. It was something quite unusual and remains an abiding memory."

For his youngest child, Hanne-Lore, Franz had always been an "authoritarian" figure. She explained: "Cuddles were with my mother."

However all four of his children would recall their excitement on the day Franz, inventive as ever, organised some fun specially for them during the exceptionally hard winter of 1947, when even the Kiel Fjord froze over.

Hanne-Lore said: "There was a frozen pond in the field where my father kept the animals. He managed to bang a hole through the ice in the middle and put in a long pole. Then he attached side poles with home-made low sledges fixed to the ends which you could sit or stand on as it was pushed round and round."

For Dieter, unexpected salvation in his daily struggle in a job he hated - and a pointer to his future career - arrived out of the blue on the day he was transferred to the ladies' department.

"I found I had a knack for styling women's hair - they used to say 'Dieter has gold in his hands!'. I didn't really know what they meant, but I was building up a reputation, so in the end I was content."

His spirits were further raised when his talent for styling secured him a prize in a hairdressing competition held in Laboe.

The flair - and easy charm - spotted early on by the ladies of Laboe was to prove the making of the young hairdresser, bringing him not only a highly successful career but also a meeting with the young woman who would change his life for ever.

By 1953, Dieter had completed his apprenticeship. Keen, like his father, to reach the highest level of his profession - Franz had been a Fleischermeister - Master Butcher - he travelled to college in Preetz each week to learn new skills.

"I used to take the ferry down to Kiel and then the bus to Preetz, about fifteen kilometres away, or in summer I would cycle all the way."

Dropping into the salon as Dieter was working one day, the kindly Otto Wulff, who had often passed him as he pedalled to college, pointed out to the young student that he could claim his travel costs from the Government.

"I had no idea that was possible, but he explained how to do it," said Dieter.

The years since he left school had been hard. However the teenager had never forgotten the advice of a visiting teacher at a meeting he attended as a young apprentice.

"He told us there was only seasonal work in Laboe, it was just a little spa town, and said: 'You must go to the Ruhr industrial region when you are qualified.'"

After considering this advice - and with his father's wise words on being independent still ringing in his ears - Dieter decided that is what he would do. His apprenticeship at last completed, he was on his way to achieving his goal of becoming a Friseurmeister - Master Hairdresser - and in April 1953, soon after his eighteenth birthday, he left Laboe to start a new life in Germany's industrial heartland.

CHAPTER 5.

BIG CITY LIFE IN ESSEN.

"I wanted to move to America to make my fortune."

When Dieter arrived in Essen on that April day in 1953, accompanied by his anxious mother, they found the city which had once symbolised the power of German industry still struggling to recover from the devastation of the Second World War.

During the conflict, tens of thousands of slave labourers had been brought in from France and other Nazi occupied countries to work in mines or in companies like Krupp's steelworks, vital for the German war effort. However Essen was a key target, and three years of concentrated Allied bombing had left the city in ruins, with ninety per cent of the centre totally destroyed.

Looking curiously around, Dieter found himself in a place like nowhere he had ever known. For amid the ruins, the rush to rebuild the infrastructure and provide new housing for the thousands who had lost their homes had turned Essen into a vast building site.

"It was very dirty, the air was dreadful, full of dust. I was always tired and always thirsty, I wanted to drink water all the time."

But the teenager was young and ambitious, keen to better himself and willing to put up with the discomforts of city life in postwar Germany.

"Now I was qualified, the future looked brighter."

He had moved in with an old friend of his father's, a medical examiner.

"He lived with his wife and son in a newly-built flat, and they agreed to provide everything I needed."

Quickly finding a hairdressing job through a newspaper advertisement, Dieter arranged to pay his hosts thirty deutsche marks each week from his forty deutsche mark salary, and set out to work towards his Master's qualification.

His new job was in Salon Hermann, in the south of the city.

"It was a much bigger, more modern salon than I was used to, with five or six staff, separate cabins for each client and even a little waiting room."

The sophisticated décor of his new workplace would leave a lasting impression on the young hairdresser, helping to form a mental picture of the salon which, he had no doubt, he himself would eventually own.

"It was very glamorous, with black walls picked out in white, white washbasins and all the fittings in light oak."

Before long, Dieter had built up his own list of clients and was experimenting with the new methods and styles which had begun to revolutionise the hairdressing industry in the postwar years.

For while older clients still clung to the carefully-sculpted waxed finger waves made popular by 1930s Hollywood film stars like Bette Davis, younger women wanted something less formal.

"Hair rollers were just coming in at that time," said Dieter, who was often asked for the popular "Harlequin" style, casually flicked up at the sides.

In Paris, London and New York, heavily back-combed "beehive" and "bouffant" styles shown in glossy fashion magazines quickly became all the rage, shaped and held in place by the new setting gels and hairspray lacquers which came onto the market in the 1950s.

It was an exciting time to be a hairdresser, banishing any lingering regrets for Dieter's original aim of working as an electrician.

Settling into his new life, he quickly developed a taste for the mussels served during the winter months at the bar next door to his workplace.

"After paying for board and lodging and for travelling to work, I had very little left over, but it was enough to treat myself a couple of times a week."

However a much-anticipated reunion with Marlis, the village blacksmith's granddaughter, a favourite playmate during her regular summer visits to Nattkischken, only underlined how far he had to go to achieve the success for which he was striving.

"She asked me how much I earned, and she couldn't believe how little it was. I realised then how different her life was. I didn't see her again."

Each day as he walked home from work through Essen's dusty streets, Dieter would pause to gaze wistfully at a place which seemed to symbolise the life which had so far eluded him.

"It was a tennis club. I could see people playing, and I was envious, wondering if I would ever have the chance to play."

If he had but known, the young man's dream was growing closer every day.

A year or so before he left Laboe, Dieter's family had finally moved out of Haus Katzbek into the ground floor of a small newly-built house in the town.

"We had just three rooms on the ground floor, so our grandmother had to find somewhere else nearby. My mother arranged to take over a new allotment so that she could continue to grow vegetables."

Meanwhile, Hilla and Walter and their children, Hans Werner and Gabriela, moved in next door.

"It was wonderful," recalled Hanne-Lore, relishing the extra space in their new home.

While he was enjoying his new-found independence, however, Dieter had always planned to bring his family to Essen to join him once he was established.

"But it was very difficult to get hold of a flat because there was so much war damage. A lot were being built, but there was always something wrong with them, partly because the coal shafts running below the city often made the ground unstable - in one, every room was out of square."

In the end, however, he secured a suitable flat through a Government agency, and the family set out to join him.

"The Government wanted as many people as possible to go to the Ruhr area to help get German industry going again," said Dieter. "They paid for them to bring everything, and so my mother, Peter, Doris and Hanne-Lore came with all the odd bits of furniture, tables and chairs they had been given, plus mattresses and even firewood."

Doris recalled: "A special train was laid on for refugees, with soup, rolls and drinks for us. Essen was already developing quite fast, so more people were needed in the mines, factories and shops."

The family's new home was on the third floor of a newly-built block of local authority flats occupied mostly by refugees like themselves.

"It was in quite a nice area, Auf der Donau, and just six minutes from Hauptbahnhof, the main station, so it was in a good position," said Dieter. "Essen was being re-designed around the station at that time - they were moving a whole cemetery to make way for it - so there was building work everywhere. Trains came right past our windows on the way to Dusseldorf but, although the air was so dusty that the sills were dirty no matter how often you cleaned them, my mother could open the window to let the sun shine in."

For Doris, by now a teenager and accustomed to the quiet countryside around Laboe, the move to the industrial Ruhr was a dramatic one.

"I wasn't scared, but Essen was a big town, full of smoke and dirt, with a lot of traffic. I knew my childhood was over, and I pined for the green meadows and seaside of Laboe."

However the bright young girl who had once been pushed to the back of the class quickly realised the advantages of the move.

"The schooling was much better, and after about six months in a secondary school, my mother heard of a special school for children with poor eyesight."

The move was to prove life-changing. Welcomed into an environment with small classes where she felt nurtured and encouraged, Doris soon began to catch up with all the years she had missed.

"Finally, I was in a place where I could flourish."

For her outgoing younger sister, however, the move to the city was simply thrilling.

"I was eleven years old, and most excited," said Hanne-Lore, who had missed her brother and always counted the days until he came home for Christmas. "I'd never been anywhere, it was something new."

For the eager young girl, even the journey to Essen proved fascinating.

"We stopped in Lübeck and were fed thick soup with pasta in it. I'd only known pasta as a sweet dish, not savoury. This was something quite different."

Still feeling the weight of responsibility for his family, Dieter was interested to note the presence of a tall man working in an office on the ground floor of their building.

"It was a centre for war reparation and his name was Fritz Streve. He had studied law at university and was sorting out pensions and so on for war widows and people injured during the war."

In fact, Fritz himself had suffered serious wounds to his face, and had lost an eye.

"I told my mother he seemed very nice, and suggested perhaps she could get together with him, maybe invite him for tea."

At forty, despite the stress of the war years, Erna remained a strikingly attractive woman, sociable and full of energy. And so, much to Dieter's satisfaction, it was not long before her relationship with Fritz blossomed, and within months the couple married.

For Doris and Hanne-Lore, the arrival of a stepfather was not altogether welcome at first. However both girls were soon won over.

"I was quite close to my mother and could talk to her about delicate matters when I grew to be a teenager, so I was wary when she married Fritz," said Hanne-Lore. "But not for long. He was a lovely, kind and learned man, and was a great help in furthering our education."

Doris agreed.

"He was a good man and like a father to me. He arranged for me to go to a kind of technical college for girls which I enjoyed very much, and I left with the all-important Certificate."

For Dieter, too, his mother's new husband brought not only a welcome lessening of his family responsibilities but also real support.

"He was better educated than us - his father had been an education director - and he was a great help to me. He was fluent in English, so he wrote all my letters for me."

After working for Salon Hermann for about a year, Dieter heard from his old boss in Laboe, Reinhold Noetsel, that he had decided to follow him to Essen and open a new salon.

"He asked me to work for him and help him set up his new business in the western part of Essen."

Ever loyal, Dieter agreed, but soon realised it had been a mistake.

"I had had my own clients at Salon Hermann, but now I had none, and I knew building up a new list would be a long haul."

Somewhat disillusioned, the ambitious young man leapt at the offer of a job with an elderly couple who said they were looking for someone to take over their salon in one of the main streets in Essen. It seemed a very good opportunity to better himself, maybe even to run his own business.

Freed from some of his family responsibilities and with his eye still firmly fixed on becoming a Friseurmeister, Dieter decided to speed up the process by taking a full-time college course.

"I could have studied in the evenings after work, but it would have taken longer, so I arranged to take three months out and do an intensive course instead."

The Hamfelde Hairdressing School was based in a small village between Lübeck and Hamburg, and for a young man whose childhood had been overshadowed by war, it would be a time to treasure.

"It was right by the forest, with a lake where you could hire boats. I had a really good time, drinking almost every night, singing with my friends. One day the teacher pointed out to me that I was wearing sunglasses in class and suggested I may be asleep or suffering from a hangover. Both were probably true."

During his time away, Dieter received a letter from his mother one day with some surprising news. It seemed his stepfather was connected to one of Germany's most illustrious families, the Mülhens, producers of the world-famous 4711 cologne.

The classic turquoise and gold bottle had become particularly familiar to wartime crews on Germany's famous U-boats when it was widely issued to try and counteract the body odour caused by lack of on-board washing facilities. In fact, it was reported that many bottles were saved, unopened, as presents for wives and girlfriends.

Erna did eventually accompany Fritz to visit his family in Cologne, the company headquarters, but, although sociable, she was a countrywoman at heart and was uncomfortable away from familiar faces and surroundings

"They always sent her a big box of cologne and other products at Christmas," recalled Dieter.

Returning to Essen with his coveted Friseurmeister certificate, Dieter resumed his job. However he soon realised that his dream of owning his own business would never come true in this salon.

"One of my colleagues told me that the owners had made the same promise to another employee in the past. When he discovered they had not been truthful, he left, so I did the same."

There followed a stint managing a hair salon on the new luxury Touropa Express train which ran through Essen. Offering travellers comfortable accommodation, fine dining and on-board hairdressing as they were whisked across the country, the elegant blue and silver train provided welcome relief from wartime deprivation and was very popular with holidaymakers in the postwar years.

But for an ambitious young man who valued his close relationships with regular clients, it proved less than satisfying.

"I didn't like it much because I only saw clients once, so I never got to know them. It was a total gypsy life. I'd come home after four or five days on the train, and in my sleep I'd still be hearing the station announcements – 'Hamburg, Bremen, Dortmund...'"

It was at this point in his life that Dieter realised the time had come to move on. Both sisters were settled in Essen and his mother had begun a new stage of her life with Fritz. Peter had recently left home to live with his girlfriend, and was working as a salesman for a cheese company in Essen, the beginning of a career at which he would excel. Once married, he would spend the rest of his life in Bavaria, the only one of Dieter's siblings to remain in Germany.

And so, weighing up his choices, Dieter, like so many others, decided that opportunity lay not in his own war-shattered country but far away across the Atlantic in America.

"It was a struggle for survival in Germany. A lot of people were emigrating to the United States, especially those from East Prussia, and I had always thought about it. One day on a train to Hamburg I met a family who were just about to go. I talked to one of their daughters and she told me about their plans. She was so excited."

Choosing not to rely on help from his Aunt Klara, still living in Pasadena, Dieter lined up a job in Chicago. First, however, he decided to go to England to learn the language.

"I planned to move to America to make my fortune, but I didn't want to be let loose there without speaking any English. Along with all the excitement and razzmatazz, I imagined it was quite a ruthless place. England seemed different, gentler and more old-fashioned."

After searching the employment columns in a hairdressing journal, he applied for a job at Jean Pierre, a salon in Tunbridge Wells in Kent owned by Swiss hairdresser Jean Pierre Ehler. He knew nothing about the town, but it was within easy reach of London, so he applied.

"Jean Pierre wrote back offering me the job, and he mentioned that he also had other stylists from what he called 'the continent'!"

And so, soon after his twenty-third birthday, Dieter set off on the longest journey of his young life.

It was a move which would have far-reaching consequences.

CHAPTER 6.

A SENSE OF HOME.

"If I was to assimilate, I knew I had to act like an Englishman."

As he walked down the gangplank after sailing from Hook of Holland into Harwich in March 1958, Dieter savoured a freedom he had not felt since his early childhood days in Nattkischken.

"It was like a stone dropping away from me - my responsibility for the rest of the family had ceased."

Stepping out of the train in London's Liverpool Street station later that morning, Dieter was immediately impressed by the droves of smartly-dressed city workers walking by in their bowler hats, briefcases in hand, umbrellas click-clicking across the busy hall.

"I had never seen these hats before, everyone seemed to be wearing them."

Hungry after his journey, he headed for a café in search of breakfast - only to be stumped by the indecipherable menu.

"I had no English at all, I hadn't even been able to prepare myself, it just wouldn't go into my brain."

What the young man did have, however, was boundless faith in his ability to make a successful life for himself in his new country.

"When you have gone through the war, somehow it energises you. I always said to myself: 'I will never be poor again', and I believed that."

Faced with the more immediate question of how to order breakfast, however, Dieter decided simply to point to the golden yellow fish being consumed by his neighbour.

"I learned later that there is a technique for eating kippers, but I had never had them before in my life, so it was a bit messy. It wasn't the first thing I would have chosen."

It had not occurred to Dieter to wonder whether he would meet a hostile reception in England, even though it was not much more than a decade since the Second World War had ended. However he was pleased to find plenty of friendly faces.

"Two ex-servicemen came to help when they realised I couldn't speak English. They had served in Germany and spoke the language, and they very kindly came with me on the underground to Charing Cross station, where I was meeting my new boss's wife."

He said: "When I got to the station, I knew straightaway who she was - she was blonde, with fancy hair."

One of the first things which struck the curious new arrival was the country's ageing cars.

"People were driving vehicles which were twenty or thirty years old. In Germany, everyone had had to give up their cars for the war effort, and they were badly damaged, so by then there were a lot of new cars on the roads. But I liked England's old cars, they were fun."

Arriving in Tunbridge Wells, Dieter found a quiet, provincial town which could not have been more different from Essen. For despite its proximity to the south coast and its front row seat during the Battle of Britain, it had remained relatively untouched by German attacks during the Second World War. Returning servicemen had found most of the town's familiar landmarks - shops and houses, schools and churches and pubs - still standing when they returned. And by now, as the 1950s drew to a close, any dust in the air came from modern developments rather than bomb site clearance.

It was arranged that the new arrival would stay at Jerningham House in Mount Sion, a small hotel close to his place of work in the historic High Street, just yards from Tunbridge Wells' famous Pantiles.

Full of youth and energy, however, he was slightly concerned to note, at breakfast the following morning, that "it looked like an old people's home, mainly elderly ladies who drank water at mealtimes".

However he soon discovered the advantages of staying there.

"The owner of that little hotel had served in the army after the war, and he spoke German. He was a great help because he would come over and talk to me."

It turned out that another guest, Dr Jameson, a retired doctor, also spoke fluent German after studying at a German university before the war.

"He was also very kind to me - I remember he bought me a diary for my new job."

Working alongside two other German speakers - one of whom was destined to remain part of his life - Dieter quickly settled in, despite a less than happy start.

"On my first day, they took me up to London to a trade fair and then to a Chinese restaurant. I had never eaten that kind of food before and that evening, when I got back the hotel, I was sick."

Fellow stylists Karl Jung, from Switzerland, and German Heinz Sneider were already established at Jean Pierre when Dieter arrived and, recalled Karl: "At first we did not embrace the new arrival. He spoke no English at all, so it was difficult for him. Heinz had become a close friend, but I had grown up during the war in Switzerland, where there was great resentment against Germans, so it took some time for me to warm to Dieter."

Still attuned to the familiar routines of his childhood, Dieter found the English habit of morning coffee breaks and afternoon tea quite alien.

"Like many other things in England, it didn't seem very efficient, but if I was to assimilate, I knew I had to act like an Englishman - and for a German, that's not easy! For us, there are no half-measures, everything has to be right. My dream was to have my own business and make my fortune, and that's something I thought about every day. I knew I would have to give up an awful lot to achieve that dream, but I never doubted I would do it. But I did get used to afternoon tea, it was rather pleasant."

However there were times, as in the early days of his apprenticeship back in Laboe, when his dream seemed very far away.

"Jean Pierre was a very up-to-date salon and I enjoyed being one of the first stylists in Tunbridge Wells to use modern hair rollers in place of the old finger waving. But some women were unhappy about it, and they even complained to Jean Pierre."

Proud to be a "modern stylist", he was "very downhearted" to hear that his cutting edge methods were not going down well with Tunbridge Wells' rather conservative older ladies.

In those early days, struggling to make his mark in a new country, it would often be the memory of the strong presence of his father, Franz, which helped to steady Dieter and keep him focussed.

"I was only fifteen when he died, but he gave me self-belief, the feeling that I could do anything."

Thankfully, Jean Pierre himself, aware of the dramatic changes sweeping through his profession, proved more far-sighted than his clients. He advised his young stylist to "carry on as you are" and in the end, to Dieter's satisfaction, many clients accustomed to having their hair styled in London switched to Jean Pierre instead.

In fact, the young German stylist so charmed one particular stockbroker's wife that she even baked his favourite German-style rye bread for him.

"She also sent me a bottle of champagne on New Year's Eve," said Dieter, chuckling to remember a time when "I was very young and perhaps a little foolish..."

After his initial spell in Jerningham House, Dieter arranged to share a flat in nearby Meadow Hill Road with colleagues Heinz and Karl.

Walking across the grassy wilderness of Tunbridge Wells Common one day, Dieter and Heinz had neared the town's celebrated Spa Hotel, high above the town, when they spotted something which brought the war years suddenly closer.

"It was a plaque marking the place where the first doodlebug fell," said Dieter. "I had heard of the V2 rockets developed in the German research centre in Peenemünde, of course, but it was so strange for us to be looking at where one had actually landed in England."

Exploring his new surroundings that summer, he was intrigued to discover tennis courts tucked away behind the quiet residential streets of old Tunbridge Wells. The famous Nevill Ground was home to Tunbridge Wells Lawn Tennis Club, one of the oldest in the country - shared with the equally renowned cricket club - and for Dieter, it offered a temptation he could not resist.

"I used to walk down there at six o'clock in the morning when there was nobody about and climb over the fence to play tennis with an Austrian au pair girl I had met. I wasn't a member, I didn't even know how to score, but I loved it."

Still keen to help his family whenever he could, Dieter arranged for his sister, Doris, now eighteen years old, to spend the summer of 1959 with him in his new home. It was a time she would never forget.

"It was one of those wonderful summers, the sun was shining every day for six weeks," said Doris, recalling long blissful hours sunbathing in her swimsuit in nearby Calverley Park.

"Everything was quite relaxed, I could grow and study, and I just fitted in."

However Doris' trip to England not only turned into the holiday of a lifetime, it also brought her into contact with the young man with whom she would spend the rest of her life.

"We just clicked," recalled Karl, looking back to the summer which would change both their lives. "She came back to England for Christmas, and we celebrated New Year at my favourite pub, the Bottle House Inn, in Chiddingstone."

The following May, Karl drove to Essen to propose to Doris and to meet her mother and stepfather. Afterwards, the newly-engaged couple travelled to Switzerland to stay with Karl's parents.

Just three months later, in August 1960, Doris and Karl were married at St Augustine's Roman Catholic Church in Tunbridge Wells.

"My mother and stepfather came over for our wedding, and Hanne-Lore was a bridesmaid," said Doris.

But as his sister's romance progressed, Dieter, too, met someone who would alter the course of his life.

Busy building his new career in Jean Pierre's salon, chatting easily to staff and clients alike, he had styled the hair of a young teacher several times when he received an unexpected invitation.

Taking up the story, Susan, his wife of sixty years, explained: "There was a Friday night dance at the Assembly Hall that day. I had been going with a boyfriend called Roger Farthing, but he hurt his ankle so I needed another partner. "

Racking her brains, she came up with the idea of inviting the friendly young stylist from Jean Pierre to accompany her.

"I liked him, we had chatted a few times as he cut my hair, but he had never been to my house."

Quickly despatched to Dieter's flat, Susan's older brother, Bernarr, left his sister's invitation with Dieter's landlady.

Susan recalled: "He turned up in a very short time, and asked what he should wear, and whether a pink shirt would do. I said, "NO!' And that was the start of it all."

Dieter - who had known full well that only a white shirt would be suitable in those more formal times, but couldn't resist the tease - agreed.

"We danced all night to Victor Sylvester without stopping, and that was it. She could dance, and we had very similar ideas about life."

In fact, unbeknown to Dieter, Susan could not only dance, she was also a top national tennis player who had been competing at the Wimbledon championships since 1954.

"I thought she was just a local club player," said Dieter. But, delighted to be invited by his new girlfriend to play at the Nevill club - no more creeping in at the crack of dawn - he quickly realised that this was no ordinary player.

"I hit the ball across the net, and she returned so hard that she knocked my racquet right out of my hand!"

The daughter of Alfred Hardwick "Hardy" Waters and his wife, Sybil, Susan was born at the family home, "Broadlands", in St John's Road, Tunbridge Wells, just a stone's throw from the club where her extraordinary gifts were first recognised.

"I used to spend all my time at St John's Tennis Club," said Susan. "My parents were both keen tennis players too, and my father was chairman of both St John's and the Nevill. By the age of nine or ten I was winning local tournaments."

Born into a wellknown local family - her paternal great-grandfather, Samuel Albert Waters, was the founder of S. Waters and Sons, a Tunbridge Wells based lettering and sign-making firm whose work was widely visible in the gold lettering on Harrods' delivery vans - Susan had been spending Christmas at "Hardwick House", her father's own childhood home just across the road, for as long as she could remember.

"My grandparents' house had a circular drive at the front and a big garden at the back with a lawn, a tennis court and orchard beyond."

Taken over by the founders' three sons after his death in 1915, the family firm was later run by Susan's father.

However it was not only the Waters who could claim deep roots in the town, for Susan's paternal grandmother, Louisa Eleanor, was the daughter of long-serving Southborough district councillor and Justice of the Peace William Edmund Hardwick.

William Hardwick, a former market gardener from Speldhurst, was not only deeply involved in local affairs, he also passed on to his only child, Susan's grandmother, a family property business which had been steadily growing over the years with the acquisition of houses in Tunbridge Wells and surrounding villages.

After working for Jean Pierre for just over a year, Dieter, keen to progress, moved to a new salon, Hunter's, opposite the old Tunbridge Wells Post Office. However the dream of owning his own salon remained, and it was not long before he began to cast around for opportunities.

For as his relationship with Susan developed, Dieter had come to a decision which would propel him in a completely new direction.

"Dieter turned to me on the steps of the salon where he was working one day and said: 'Let's spend the rest of our lives together,'" said Susan. "I had no hesitation in accepting."

It was a union which would bring together two very different lives, one lived in the heart of middle England, the other begun hundreds of miles away in a land doomed to be erased from the map.

For Susan, whose brother Bernarr - named for American health and fitness pioneer Bernarr Macfadden - had liked to poke fun at her clutch of local boyfriends, Dieter brought a beguiling energy and a sense of certainty which made him stand out from the young men she had known for most of her life.

And for Dieter, invited to Susan's family home for the first time, the late Victorian house in Boyne Park, with its solid redbrick walls and family portraits all around, was a haven of peace and security.

"We had lost everything in Memelland, so I really liked this old house where things had stayed the same. It was so secure and well built - little did I realise that I would own it myself one day."

They were married just after Christmas 1960 at the bride's own church, St Paul's in Rusthall. For the second time in less than a year, Erna found herself celebrating the marriage of one of her children hundreds of miles from her home and, again, Hanne-Lore was a bridesmaid.

For Karl, who at first had known nothing of his flatmate's romance, it was a union so unlikely that he had serious doubts about its success.

"My wife was German too, but I just couldn't understand how Susan's parents could accept Dieter. But it was their affair, not mine, and of course everything did work out well."

Dieter, too, was aware that Susan's decision to marry a German may not have been welcomed by her parents.

"Of course, the war was still very recent. But Susan's father had been to Hamburg before the war and met some nice Germans who were embarrassed by Hitler, so he understood. But I had a feeling my mother-in-law didn't like me, I think she thought I was too robust. I had seen how quietly most people said their wedding vows, so when we got married I boomed: 'I DO!' I could see people looking at each other!"

However the birth of a grandchild the following autumn would bring Sybil round for, noted Dieter, "they knew I would look after their daughter".

The young couple began their married life in the Waters' roomy family home. At this time, Susan, whose schooldays had been spent at Hamilton House School in Tunbridge Wells and later at Tonbridge Girls' Grammar School, was teaching PE at a local Roman Catholic girls' school, Beechwood Sacred Heart.

"I had moved away to train at Dartford College of Physical Education and then to teach in Purley, but I was pleased to be back in Tunbridge Wells," said Susan. "I always assumed I would spend my life here."

So now, with his early plan to move to America cast aside without regret, Dieter set about finding somewhere to start his business.

He said: "I had saved up quite a lot of money and we had already bought a house being built in Pembury. One day Susan and I went for a drive to Hawkhurst, and I came across a former fish shop next to a pub just outside the village. It was for sale and I bought it straight away for £2,300. Susan was a bit surprised and people warned me it was a risk, but I just knew it was right."

Within weeks, the Dieter Henry salon was up and running.

"Hair salons at that time were very basic, not very attractive. I wanted mine to be different from everyone else's," said Dieter, recalling the fashionable cream padded desk at the small reception area at the front, fresh flowers brought in from their own Tunbridge Wells garden and the rich red velvet curtain draped across less-than-perfect walls.

"I started in 1961 with one apprentice, seven chairs and a plastic chandelier - I couldn't afford a real one - and I created an archway through to a room at the back, because I knew I would be expanding."

In the early months, as they waited for their first house to be completed, Dieter and Susan lived above the shop. As well as manning the reception desk when teaching commitments allowed, Susan also took on all the administration of the business, later recalling the day when, hours after giving birth to Richard, their first child, she found herself sorting out staff wages.

"I couldn't have built the business without her," said Dieter, whose childhood battle with dyslexia remained.

And so began the most fruitful period of his life, the time when he was able to realise his dreams and begin to build the safe, secure life which had dominated his dreams for so long.

"On the first Saturday morning we had just one client, but within four months we were full. Ladies started to come in from Tunbridge Wells and also London people with country houses in the area, some of them quite famous."

As the business grew, staff increased, and eventually Dieter was able to extend the building and create a bright, modern salon in tune with changing times.

"I brought in four swinging washbasins from Germany - you lose up to five minutes every time a client has to move from her seat to have her hair washed - moveable hairdryers, specially-made mirrors and cork floors. Sometimes on a winter afternoon I would just stand outside to see all the lights shining in my salon, it was very satisfying."

For one member of staff, however, Dieter's energy proved a little too much.

"She was a middle-aged lady and she said to me one day: 'Mr Dieter, I've got to leave you. You make me dizzy!'"

Always thinking and planning, on fine days he would often wander down the road past nearby fields to a little footbridge where he could sit quietly and gather his thoughts.

"I would think about my clients and about how I could improve things, because nothing is ever perfect."

As his business prospered, Dieter came up with the idea of buying "Westbourne", Susan's parents' house, for his growing family, which by 1966 would include two more sons, Philip and James, and daughter Sarah.

"It hadn't occurred to me before, and no-one took me seriously at first. But my business was going extremely well, and I was able to pay the going rate, so I proved them wrong. Big Victorian houses like this were not popular at the time, but it gave me great joy."

After some discussion, it was agreed that a plot of land in the spacious garden would be handed over to Susan's parents so that they could build a new house for themselves nearby.

Trying to balance work and family life, always with an eye to future opportunities, there was one nagging subject which had continued to hover at the back of Dieter's mind - the fate of Bronislawa Deptula, one of the maids who worked for his family. He had heard nothing from his much-loved childhood companion since the day the teenager left to visit her parents in Poland in the early years of the war, and had no idea whether she had survived.

"I always wondered what had happened to her, and so in the end I put an advertisement in a Polish newspaper. Her granddaughter, a student, saw it and showed it to her, and she recognised my name immediately."

To his great joy, Dieter was finally able to meet up with his old friend. Now widowed, she lived north of Warsaw in the old town of Pultusk, close to her children and grandchildren. It was then, at an emotional reunion, that he learned she had been arrested on arrival back in Poland and forced to work in a factory.

In 1980, after almost twenty successful years in Hawkhurst, Dieter decided to sell the business to make way for a fresh challenge. It was a move which, a decade after his successful application for British citizenship, would bring him even closer to the heart of his adopted country.

Having decided to launch a new salon in Tunbridge Wells itself, he came across Romary House, a four-storey family home in Church Road just a stone's throw from both the Common and the Town Hall.

"I had a good feeling about it," said Dieter who, as ever, wasted no time in putting his plan into action.

But as work began to turn the old house into a modern salon, with equipment brought in from Germany, he was thrilled to learn that his new base carried a name once famous across the world. For it was here, over a century earlier, that Alfred Romary had begun to bake the celebrated wafer biscuits which would become a favourite with Queen Victoria herself. And when the queen honoured the company with a Royal Warrant, their biscuits soon appeared in top London stores like Harrods and Fortnum and Mason as well as places as far afield as New York and Paris.

But despite Dieter's faith in his vision, establishing his business, Romary House Hairdressing International, in a conservative town like Tunbridge Wells proved a challenge.

"It wasn't easy, there was plenty of competition, but I made a lot of improvements and eventually we were working on three floors."

But despite the success of his latest salon, Dieter had decided long ago that hairdressing was a young man's game.

He said: "It is an industry which is changing all the time, and you must change with it. I always felt that by the age of fifty I would have reached the end of the period of great creativity and so, within a few years, I had decided to retire."

However there was another, equally compelling reason why Dieter was content to leave his hairdressing days behind him. After some encouragement from Alfred Waters, his father-in-law, he had agreed to join the family property business passed down through the generations from William Edmund Hardwick, Susan's great-grandfather.

Dieter explained: "Susan's father and his sisters, Doris and Gwendolin, had inherited properties in and around Tunbridge Wells through their mother, Louisa. But Hardy was more of an intellectual than a businessman, he believed in moderation in all things, and he had mentioned several times that perhaps I could take them on. But I told him: 'I don't know anything about it, hairdressing is what I know about.'"

Eventually, however, the challenge sparked his imagination and, once involved, he had set about bringing the portfolio of ageing cottages and houses up to date.

He said: "There were forty houses on controlled rents, a lot of them very old-fashioned, with outside toilets and leaking roofs, and some even had old 'copper' boilers for washing. I wanted to improve them to make the business more efficient, but also because I know what it's like to have nothing, and I had a real urge to look after the tenants. That was something which gave me great satisfaction."

In time, the growing business would also employ two of Dieter's own sons, Richard and James, adding another generation to the story.

Looking back on his long life some sixty years after his first arrival in the country which would become his home, Dieter said: "I've had a good life. It has been tough, but I've learned an awful lot about human behaviour. There have been difficulties along the way, and of course you have to make sacrifices, but I have never doubted myself."

Some years ago, a bizarre meeting in the grounds of Chartwell, Winston Churchill's famous home in Kent, served to underline the distance travelled by the boy from Memelland.

Dieter recalled: "I had hurt my knee, so I was walking with a stick, wearing a panama hat and gloves and smoking a cigar. I saw a group of people coming towards me and suddenly a chap jumped out and said in an American accent: 'Gee Mr Churchill, I'm so glad to meet with you!'"

Summoning his best British accent, Dieter asked: "Are you having a good time on my estate?" and walked briskly on, swinging his stick, trying not to laugh out loud.

POSTSCRIPT

In 1991, following the break-up of the Soviet Union, Dieter Teubler returned to the scene of his boyhood for the first time.

It was forty-seven years since he and his family had fled from their farm in Nattkischken and, while Memelland itself had vanished into Lithuania in the postwar shake-up of Europe, he and his step-sister, Hilla, found a great deal which was familiar.

Approaching their old home along the road lined by the silver birches remembered from his childhood, he saw the farmhouse still standing alongside his father's sausage workshop. However much had changed.

"We both broke down when we got to the house," said Dieter. "It was hard, the changes were so dramatic. After the war, the Russians had got rid of all the little farms like ours to make a big collective farm, with large-scale milk production."

In the once-spacious farmhouse, rooms had been divided to accommodate several families, and Franz Teubler's brick-built workshop, where his famous sausages were produced and sold throughout the area, had also been turned into living accommodation.

Later, Dieter visited Nattkischken again, this time with his family.

He said: "It was important to me for my children and grandchildren to know their roots, to understand where they came from."

Before they left, the family visited the memorial erected by Dieter and other members of his generation on the site of the old village church, which was destroyed during the war.

The inscription reads: "Gott gieb uns die Kraft zu akzeptieren was wir nicht ändern können" - God give us strength to accept what we cannot change.

INDEX

Printed in Great Britain
by Amazon

23883550R00066